혼공

기초영문법

혼공 허준석 지음

L1

혼공 기초 영문법 Level 1

1판 1쇄 2022년 2월 7일
1판 6쇄 2025년 1월 6일

지은이   허준석
표지디자인 박새롬
내지디자인 황지영
표지그림 김효지
마케팅   두잉글 사업본부
브랜드   혼공북스
펴낸곳   혼공북스
출판등록 제2021-000288호
주   소   04033 서울특별시 마포구 양화로 113 4층(서교동)
전자메일 team@hongong.co.kr

ISBN   979-11-976810-3-5   13740

혼공!

영어 공부 참 어렵습니다. 특히, 영문법이란 말을 들으면 어디서부터 시작해야 할지 앞이 깜깜합니다. 저 역시도 그러한 경험을 했었기에, 세상에서 가장 쉽게 영문법 공부를 할 수 있는 책이나 강의가 있으면 좋겠다고 생각을 했습니다. 그래서, 혼공 기초 영문법이 탄생했습니다. 짧은 이론, 반복되는 개념, 쓰기 위주의 연습을 통해 그 동안 공부해오던 방식을 벗어날 수 있을 것입니다.

영문법에는 규칙도 많고, 예외도 참 많습니다. 많은 사람들은 예외를 보면서 겁에 질려 영어 공부를 중단하게 됩니다. 그럴 필요 없습니다. 왜 규칙이 생겼는지 이해하고, 조금 외우고, 예외는 이런 게 있구나 하고 넘어가도 됩니다. 이렇게 반복해서 학습하다보면 애쓰지 않아도 예외까지 완벽하게 익혀지게 됩니다. 반대로, 처음부터 예외를 파고들어 공부한다면, 실수할까봐 영어로 말하기도 쓰기도 제대로 못하게 됩니다.

혼공 영어는 결국 말하고, 실전에서 쓸 수 있는 영어를 목표로 하고 있습니다. 쉽게 공부해서 자신감을 찾고, 점점 더 깊이 있는 공부를 하면서 내가 원하는 영어 실력에 도달하길 바랍니다. 재미있게 끝까지 간다면 무조건 성공합니다. 끈기를 가지고 혼공하세요!

혼공 허준석 드림

오리엔테이션

💡 **혼공개념** | 8품사

품사란?

모든 영단어는 영어로 된 문장 속에서 각자의 역할이 있답니다. 영어에서는 총 8가지 품사가 있습니다.

1 명사

사람, 장소, 사물을 부를 때 쓰는 단어랍니다.

예 Jason, McDonald's, chair...

2 대명사

같은 명사를 반복해서 부르는 것을 막기 위해 쓰는 단어랍니다.

예 he, him, his, it, that...

3 동사

사람이나 사물의 움직임이나 상태를 전해주기 위해 쓰는 단어랍니다.

예 like, run, eat, see...

4 형용사

명사를 좀 더 구체적으로 설명해주는 단어랍니다.

예 handsome, young, old...

5 부사

동사, 형용사, 부사 또는 문장 전체의 의미를 구체적으로 만들어주는 단어랍니다.

예 now, slowly, very...

6 전치사

주로 시간, 장소, 기타를 표현하기 위해 명사와 덩어리를 이루어 쓰이는 단어랍니다.

예 at, on, in, for...

7 접속사

말을 좀 더 길게 하고 싶을 때 쓰는 단어로, '단어와 단어', '문장과 문장' 등을 연결합니다.

예 and, but, because, that...

8 감탄사

기쁨, 놀라움, 슬픔 등의 감정을 나타내는 단어입니다.

예 oh, oops, hooray...

💡 **혼공개념** | 문장 만들기

한국어 어순보다 사실은 더 쉬운 게 영어 어순이랍니다. '머리 - 몸통' + 나머지의 순서로 그림 그리듯 나가면 됩니다.

1 주어 + 동사

예 I meet.

2 주어 + 동사 + 의미1

예 I meet Tom.

3 주어 + 동사 + 의미1 + 의미2

예 I meet Tom at 11.

contents

00 오리엔테이션 4

01 명사의 수 11
    셀 수 있는 명사, 셀 수 없는 명사, 명사의 종류

02 명사의 복수형태 만들기 15
    명사의 복수 형태 만드는 방법, There is / are ~

03 인칭대명사의 주격 / 소유격 19
    격의 개념, 인칭대명사의 주격, 소유격, 명사의 소유격

04 인칭대명사의 목적격 23
    인칭대명사의 목적격, 명사의 목적격

05 소유대명사 27
    소유대명사의 개념, 명사의 소유대명사

06 be동사의 현재형 31
    be동사 현재형의 개념, 문장에서의 사용, 부정

07 be동사의 과거형 35
    be동사 과거형의 개념, 문장에서의 사용, 부정

08 be동사의 의문문 39
    be동사 의문문의 어순, 대답하기

09 지시대명사 / 지시형용사 43
    지시대명사 / 지시형용사 this, that, these, those / 의문문 만들기

10 일반동사의 현재형 1 47
    일반동사 현재형의 개념, 일반동사 + s, es

11 일반동사의 현재형 2 ⸺⸺⸺⸺⸺⸺⸺ 51
일반동사의 부정, 현재진행형

12 일반동사의 과거형 1 ⸺⸺⸺⸺⸺⸺⸺ 55
일반동사의 규칙 과거형 4가지

13 일반동사의 과거형 2 ⸺⸺⸺⸺⸺⸺⸺ 59
일반동사의 불규칙 과거형

14 일반동사의 과거형 3 ⸺⸺⸺⸺⸺⸺⸺ 63
일반동사 과거형 부정하기, 과거 진행형

15 일반동사의 의문문 ⸺⸺⸺⸺⸺⸺⸺ 67
일반동사의 의문문 만들기, 의문문에 대답하기

16 부정관사 / 정관사 ⸺⸺⸺⸺⸺⸺⸺ 71
부정관사 a, an, 정관사 the

17 의문사 의문문 ⸺⸺⸺⸺⸺⸺⸺ 75
who, what, when, where, why, how, which, whose,
의문사 + 형용사, 의문사 + 명사

18 부가의문문 ⸺⸺⸺⸺⸺⸺⸺ 79
부가의문문 만들기, 대답하기

19 조동사 can ⸺⸺⸺⸺⸺⸺⸺ 83
can의 의미, 부정하기, 의문문, 부가의문문

20 조동사 will ⸺⸺⸺⸺⸺⸺⸺ 87
will의 의미, 부정하기, 여러 가지 축약형, 의문문

contents

21 조동사 may ———————————————— 91
    may의 의미, 부정하기, 의문문

22 조동사 must ——————————————— 95
    must의 의미, 부정하기, 의문문

23 형용사의 용법————————————————— 99
    형용사의 개념, 한정적 용법, 서술적 용법

24 수량 형용사 1 ——————————————— 103
    many, much, a lot of(lots of), How many / How much

25 수량 형용사 2 ——————————————— 107
    few, a few, little, a little, some, any

26 부사 / 빈도부사 ——————————————— 111
    부사의 개념, 형태, 빈도부사의 개념과 종류

27 what / how 감탄문 ————————————— 115
    감탄문의 원리, 문장구조

28 비인칭 주어 it ——————————————— 119
    비인칭 주어의 개념, 쓰이는 상황

29 시간을 나타내는 전치사 ————————————— 123
    시간을 나타내는 at, in, on

30 장소를 나타내는 전치사 ————————————— 127
    장소를 나타내는 다양한 전치사들

    정답 ———————————————————— 131

혼공 기초 영문법
LEVEL 1

혼공 기초 영문법
LEVEL 1

명사의 수

> 💡 **혼공개념** | 셀 수 있는/없는 명사란?

1 셀 수 있는 명사 : 명사 앞에 one, two, three...등 숫자를 붙여 셀 수 있는 명사

예 apple, car, book, flower, ball, computer...

2 셀 수 없는 명사 : 여러 가지 이유로 숫자를 붙여 셀 수 없는 명사

1) 추상명사 : 형태가 없어 눈에 보이지 않는 명사

예 beauty, luck, friendship, happiness, love

2) 고유명사 : 사람이나 사물의 이름

예 Jun, Kevin, Chloe, Han River

3) 물질명사 : 액체나 덩어리, 조각으로 이루어진 것

예 water, milk, bread, cheese, paper, gold

혼공 팁

물질명사는 <u>a glass of</u> milk(water), <u>a cup of</u> coffee, <u>a piece(sheet) of</u> paper,
<u>two slices of</u> cheese(bread)와 같이 단위(glass, cup, loaf, piece, sheet, slice...)를 써서 센다.

4) 기타 여러 종류를 포함하는 것

예 furniture, luggage, money...

혼공 연습

A 다음 단어 중 셀 수 없는 명사에 동그라미를 치시오.

① apple   water

② bread   book

③ computer   luggage

④ money   ball

⑤ flower   Chloe

β 다음 셀 수 없는 명사들 중 성질이 다른 하나에 동그라미를 치시오.

① Jun   beauty   luck

② Jason   Han River   water

③ milk   love   paper

④ furniture   bread   gold

⑤ money   luggage   cheese

⑥ friendship   Kevin   happiness

⑦ water   paper   furniture

A 다음 상자에 있는 단어들을 셀 수 있는 명사와 셀 수 없는 명사로 구분하시오.

apple	milk	water	money	banana	beauty
ham	child	cheese	sugar	salt	paper
love	pride	courage	happiness	furniture	computer

셀 수 있는 명사	셀 수 없는 명사

B 다음 우리말을 보고 빈칸에 알맞은 단어를 쓰시오.

① 국에 <u>달걀 두 개</u>를 넣으세요.

Put _____ _____ in the soup.

② Tom에게 <u>행운</u>을 빈다!

Good _____ to Tom!

③ 나는 약간의 <u>물</u>과 <u>우유</u>가 필요해요.

I need some _____ and _____.

④ <u>빵 한 덩어리</u>와 <u>치즈 두 장</u>

a _____ of _____ and _____ _____ of _____

A. 다음 단어들을 보고 ①번의 예시처럼 빈칸을 채우시오.

	단어		의미	셀 수 있음
①	apple	apple	사과	○
②	milk			
③	water			
④	money			
⑤	banana			
⑥	beauty			
⑦	flower			
⑧	cheese			
⑨	sugar			
⑩	salt			
⑪	paper			
⑫	love			
⑬	pride			
⑭	courage			
⑮	happiness			
⑯	furniture			
⑰	Kevin			
⑱	ball			
⑲	gold			
⑳	luggage			
㉑	computer			
㉒	ham			

정답 ② 우유(X)   ③ 물(X)   ④ 돈(X)   ⑤ 바나나(O)   ⑥ 미, 아름다움(X)   ⑦ 꽃(O)   ⑧ 치즈(X)   ⑨ 설탕(X)   ⑩ 소금(X)   ⑪ 종이(X)   ⑫ 사랑(X)
⑬ 자부심(X)   ⑭ 용기(X)   ⑮ 행복(X)   ⑯ 가구(X)   ⑰ 케빈(X)   ⑱ 공(O)   ⑲ 금(X)   ⑳ 짐(X)   ㉑ 컴퓨터(O)   ㉒ 햄(X)

명사의 복수형태 만들기

💡 혼공개념 명사의 단수, 복수란?

단수	복수
하나의 명사	두 개 이상의 명사
one apple	two apples

혼공 팁

명사의 복수 만드는 방법

① 명사 + s : boats, hats, carrots ...

② -s, -ss, -x, -ch, -sh, -o로 끝나는 명사 + es :
buses, dresses, axes, churches, dishes, potatoes   주의 piano→pianos

③ 모음 + y로 끝나는 명사 + s : days, boys, toys, monkeys

④ 자음 + y로 끝나는 명사 ⇒ y를 i로 바꾸고 + es :
fly→flies, city→cities, baby→babies

⑤ -f, -fe로 끝나는 명사 ⇒ f, fe를 v로 바꾸고 + es :
leaf→leaves, knife→knives, wolf→wolves

⑥ 항상 짝을 이루어야 하는 명사는 늘 복수로 쓴다 :
glasses, scissors, pants, chopsticks, pajamas...

⑦ 위의 규칙과 관계없는 것들은 불규칙이라 부른다 :
man→men, child→children, tooth→teeth, foot→feet

💡 혼공개념 There is / are

1 의미: ~가 있다(발견)

There is + 단수명사	There are + 복수명사
There is an apple.	There are two apples.

Part 1

혼공 연습

A 다음 영단어의 복수 형태를 적으시오.

① boat _____ hat _____ carrot _____

② bus _____ class _____ ax _____

③ church _____ dish _____ potato _____

④ day _____ boy _____ toy _____

⑤ monkey _____ fly _____ city _____

⑥ baby _____ leaf _____ knife _____

⑦ man _____ child _____ tooth _____

⑧ foot _____ woman _____

B 다음 우리말을 보고 빈칸에 알맞은 단어를 쓰시오.

① 안경 - _____

② 가위 - _____

③ 바지 - _____

④ 젓가락 - _____

⑤ 잠옷 - _____

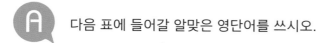

A 다음 표에 들어갈 알맞은 영단어를 쓰시오.

a dress	dresses
a family	
a bench	
a woman	

B 다음 사진을 보고 알맞은 표현을 영어로 쓰시오.

① three a_____   ② two _____   ③ _____ l_____

C 다음 문장의 밑줄 친 부분을 올바르게 고치시오.

① There are two <u>pianoes</u> in the room.

② I need 10 <u>potato</u>!

③ I like my <u>pajama</u>.

④ There are seven <u>day</u> in a week.

A. 다음 단어들을 보고 ①번의 예시처럼 빈칸을 채우시오.

	단수	복수		단수	복수		단수	복수
①	boat	boats	⑪	woman		㉑	baby	
②	carrot		⑫	tooth		㉒	knife	
③	class		⑬	hat		㉓	child	
④	church		⑭	bus		㉔	piano	
⑤	potato		⑮	ax		㉕	tooth	
⑥	boy		⑯	dish		㉖	foot	
⑦	monkey		⑰	day		㉗	dress	
⑧	city		⑱	toy		㉘	family	
⑨	leaf		⑲	fly		㉙	wolf	
⑩	man		⑳	bench				

B. 다음 항상 짝을 이루어야 하는 명사의 우리말 의미를 적으시오.

㉚	glasses		㉝	chopsticks	
㉛	scissors		㉞	pajamas	
㉜	pants				

C. 우리말 힌트를 참고하여 빈칸에 알맞은 형태의 명사를 적으시오.

㉟ There are two _____ in the room. (피아노)

㊱ I need 10 _____! (감자)

㊲ I like my _____. (잠옷)

㊳ There are seven _____ in a week. (일)

정답 ② carrots ③ classes ④ churches ⑤ potatoes ⑥ boys ⑦ monkeys ⑧ cities ⑨ leaves ⑩ men ⑪ women ⑫ teeth ⑬ hats ⑭ buses ⑮ axes ⑯ dishes ⑰ days ⑱ toys ⑲ flies ⑳ benches ㉑ babies ㉒ knives ㉓ children ㉔ pianos ㉕ teeth ㉖ feet ㉗ dresses ㉘families ㉙ wolves ㉚ 안경 ㉛ 가위 ㉜ 바지 ㉝ 젓가락 ㉞잠옷 ㉟ pianos ㊱ potatoes ㊲ pajamas ㊳ days

인칭대명사의 주격 / 소유격

💡 혼공개념 격, 인칭대명사의 주격, 소유격이란?

1 ~격 : 문장에서 단어가 있는 자리

2 주격: 주어 자리에 온 단어(~은, 는, 이, 가)

예 I, he, she...

3 소유격: 명사 앞에서 '~의'라는 의미를 가진 단어

예 my, your, his, her...

혼공 팁

반드시 주격, 소유격은 자신의 자리에 쓰여야 한다.

예 I love my story. (O)   My love I story. (X)
    나는   나의   나의   나는

💡 혼공개념 명사의 주격, 소유격

1 명사의 주격: 명사 형태 그대로 씀

예 Jerry is cute.

2 명사의 소유격: 명사 + 's

예 John's friends

구분	단수		복수	
	주격	소유격	주격	소유격
1인칭	I	my	we	our
2인칭	you	your	you	your
3인칭	he	his	they	their
	she	her		
	it	its		

A 다음 우리말을 보고 빈칸에 알맞은 영어 단어를 쓰시오.

① 나는(난) _____ _____   나의(내) _____ _____

② 너는(넌) _____ _____   너의(네) _____ _____

③ 그는   _____ _____   그의   _____ _____

④ 그녀는   _____ _____   그녀의   _____ _____

⑤ 그것은   _____ _____   그것의   _____ _____

⑥ 우리들은 _____ _____   우리들의 _____ _____

⑦ 너희들은 _____ _____   너희들의 _____ _____

⑧ 그들은   _____ _____   그들의   _____ _____

β 다음 우리말 문장의 밑줄 친 부분을 의미에 맞는 영단어로 쓰시오.

① 내 동생은 열 살이다.   _____

② 너의 키는 170cm이다.   _____

③ 넌 언젠가 꿈을 이룰 수 있을 것이다.   _____

④ 그는 그녀의 자동차를 좋아한다.   _____ _____

⑤ 그녀는 그의 프러포즈를 받아들였다.   _____ _____

⑥ 그것은 Joe의 전 재산이다.   _____

⑦ 우리들은 그것의 핵심을 파악하지 못했다.   _____ _____

⑧ Jason은 그들의 심부름을 해야 한다.   _____ _____

A 괄호 안의 우리말을 참고하여 빈칸에 알맞은 영단어를 쓰시오.

① _____ is expensive. (그것은)

② _____ am from Seoul. (나는)

③ _____ likes sheep. (그녀는)

④ I love _____ watch. (그녀의)

⑤ _____ love _____ story. (나는, 그녀의)

⑥ _____ are _____ cats. (그것들은, 그의)

⑦ _____ and _____ sister like bananas. (그는, 그의)

⑧ _____ like _____ color. (그들은, 그것의)

B 다음 우리말을 보고 빈칸에 알맞은 단어를 쓰시오.

① 이것은 그녀의 연필이다.

This is _____ pencil.

② 저것은 Kevin의 자동차이다.

That is _____ car.

③ Kevin은 그의 자동차를 좋아한다.

_____ likes _____ car.

④ 나는 그들의 음악을 정말 좋아한다.

_____ really like _____ music.

A. 다음 빈칸을 예시처럼 채우시오.

구분	단수		복수	
	주격	소유격	주격	소유격
1인칭	I	my		
2인칭				
3인칭				

B. 다음 우리말을 보고 빈칸에 알맞은 단어를 쓰시오.

① 이것은 그녀의 연필이다.

　 This is _____ pencil.

② 저것은 Kevin의 자동차이다.

　 That is _____ car.

③ Kevin은 그의 자동차를 좋아한다.

　 _____ likes _____ car.

④ 나는 그들의 음악을 정말 좋아한다.

　 _____ really like _____ music.

정답 A의 정답은 앞 페이지의 오늘 공부했던 박스를 참고하세요. ① her ② Kevin's ③ Kevin, his ④ I, their

인칭대명사의 목적격

💡 혼공개념 | 목적격이란?

1 목적격: 주로 '~을, 를' 이란 의미로 해석됨(때때로 '~에게' 라는 의미로 쓰이기도 함)

예 him(그를), her(그녀를)...

혼공 팁

주격은 '~은, 는, 이, 가', 소유격은 '~의'라고 해석되는 단어이다. 따라서, 목적격 단어와 바꿔서 쓰면 안 된다.

예 Chloe likes <u>him</u>. (O)   Chole likes <u>he</u>. (X)
          그를   그는

💡 혼공개념 | 명사의 목적격이란?

1 명사의 목적격: 주격처럼 원래 형태로 쓰며 '~을, 를'을 붙여 해석함

예 She likes <u>Tom</u>. (O)   <u>Tom</u> likes her. (O)
    Tom을(목적격)   Tom은(주격)

구분	단수			복수		
	주격	소유격	목적격	주격	소유격	목적격
1인칭	I	my	me	we	our	us
2인칭	you	your	you	you	your	you
3인칭	he	his	him	they	their	them
	she	her	her			
	it	its	it			

A 다음 우리말을 보고 알맞은 영어 단어를 빈칸에 쓰시오.

① 나는(난) _____ _____   나를(날) _____ _____

② 너는(넌) _____ _____   너를(널) _____ _____

③ 그의 _____ _____   그를 _____ _____

④ 그녀의 _____ _____   그녀를 _____ _____

⑤ 그것은 _____ _____   그것을 _____ _____

⑥ 우리들은 _____ _____   우리들을 _____ _____

⑦ 너희들의 _____ _____   너희들을 _____ _____

⑧ 그들의 _____ _____   그들을 _____ _____

β 다음 우리말 문장의 밑줄 친 부분을 의미에 맞는 영단어로 쓰시오.

① 나는 그를 좋아한다. _____

② 그는 그것을 먹는다. _____

③ 그녀는 우리들을 데리고 갈 것이다. _____

④ 그는 그들을 반겨줄 것이다. _____ _____

⑤ 그녀는 그것을 받아들였다. _____ _____

⑥ 그것은 Joe를 나타낸다. _____ _____

⑦ Kevin은 너를 찾지 못할 것이다. _____ _____

⑧ 그들은 Jason을 보호해야 한다. _____ _____

A 우리말 힌트를 참고하여 빈칸에 알맞은 영단어를 쓰시오.

① I like _____. (그들을)

② He loves _____. (나를)

③ Please help _____. (우리들을)

④ Tom likes _____. (그녀를)

⑤ _____ respect _____. (나는, Mr. Kim을)

⑥ _____ helps _____. (그녀는, 너를)

⑦ _____ and _____ sister like _____. (그는, 그의, 그것을)

⑧ _____ brothers eat _____. (그녀의, 그것들을)

β 다음 우리말 의미를 참고하여 빈칸을 채우시오.

① 지후는 그녀를 좋아한다.

Jihoo likes _____.

② 나는 그것을 아침에 먹는다.

I eat _____ in the morning.

③ 그들을 봐.

Look at _____.

④ 그녀는 우리들을 존경한다.

_____ respects _____.

A. 다음 빈칸을 예시처럼 채우시오.

구분	단수			복수		
	주격	소유격	목적격	주격	소유격	목적격
1인칭	I	my	me			
2인칭						
3인칭						

B. 다음 밑줄 친 부분을 영어로 쓰시오.

① 나는 <u>그를</u> 좋아한다. _____

② 그녀는 <u>우리들을</u> 데리고 갈 것이다. _____

③ 그는 <u>그들을</u> 반겨줄 것이다. _____

④ 그것은 <u>Joe</u>를 나타낸다. _____

C. 다음 우리말을 보고 빈칸에 알맞은 단어를 쓰시오.

⑤ 나는 그것을 아침에 먹는다.

_____ eat _____ in the morning.

⑥ 그녀는 그들을 돕는다.

_____ helps _____.

소유대명사

소유대명사란?

1 소유대명사의 의미: ~의 것('나의 것'을 제외하고는 대부분 소유격의 형태 + s)

예 It is yours. (O)　　　　It is your. (X)
　　　너의 것　　　　　　　　너의

2 명사의 소유대명사 만드는 방법: 명사 + 's

예 It is Jimmy's.
　　　지미의 것

혼공 팁

사람 이름의 소유격은 소유대명사와 형태가 같으니 유의해야 한다.

예 It is Mike's house.(소유격)　　　It is Mike's.(소유대명사)

구분	단수				복수			
	주격	소유격	목적격	소유대명사	주격	소유격	목적격	소유대명사
1인칭	I	my	me	mine	we	our	us	ours
2인칭	you	your	you	yours	you	your	you	yours
3인칭	he	his	him	his	they	their	them	theirs
	she	her	her	hers				
	it	its	it	없음				

A 다음 우리말을 보고 알맞은 영어 단어를 빈칸에 쓰시오.

① 나의(내) _____ _____ 나의(내) 것 _____ _____

② 너를(널) _____ _____ 너의(네) 것 _____ _____

③ 그의 _____ _____ 그의 것 _____ _____

④ 그녀를 _____ _____ 그녀의 것 _____ _____

⑤ 그것의 _____ _____ 그것을 _____ _____

⑥ 우리들을 _____ _____ 우리들의 것 _____ _____

⑦ 너희들은 _____ _____ 너희들의 것 _____ _____

⑧ 그들을 _____ _____ 그들의 것 _____ _____

B 다음 우리말 문장의 밑줄 친 부분을 의미에 맞는 영단어로 쓰시오.

① 이것은 <u>나의 것</u>이다. _____

② 저것은 <u>그녀의 것</u>이니? _____

③ 이 장난감은 <u>너의 것</u>이다. _____

④ 이 집은 <u>그의 것</u>이다. _____

⑤ 밖에 주차된 자전거들은 <u>우리들의 것</u>이다. _____

⑥ 이 자동차들은 <u>그들의 것</u>이다. _____

⑦ <u>내 것</u>이 곧 <u>그녀의 것</u>이다. _____ _____

A 우리말 힌트를 참고하여 빈칸에 알맞은 영단어를 쓰시오.

① This is _____. (나의 것)

② Is this _____? (너의 것)

③ Look at _____. (그들의 것)

④ Jason likes _____. (그의 것)

⑤ _____ eats _____. (그는, 우리들의 것)

⑥ _____ is _____. (그것, 그들의 것)

⑦ This doll is _____. (그녀의 것)

β 다음 우리말 의미를 참고하여 빈칸을 채우시오.

① 저 집은 그들의 것이다.

   That house is _____.

② 저 일기장은 그녀의 것이다.

   That diary is _____.

③ 이 정원은 우리들의 것이다.

   This garden is _____.

④ 그 책들은 나의 것이다.

   The books are _____.

혼공복습

A. 다음 빈칸을 예시처럼 채우시오.

구분	단수				복수			
	주격	소유격	목적격	소유대명사	주격	소유격	목적격	소유대명사
1인칭	I	my	me	mine				
2인칭								
3인칭								

B. 다음 밑줄 친 우리말을 영어로 쓰시오.

① 저것은 <u>그녀의 것</u>이니?　　　＿＿＿＿＿＿

② 이 집은 <u>그의 것</u>이다.　　　＿＿＿＿＿＿

③ 이 장난감은 <u>너의 것</u>이다.　　＿＿＿＿＿＿

C. 다음 우리말을 보고 빈칸에 알맞은 단어를 쓰시오.

④ 저 집은 그들의 것이다.

　　That house is ＿＿＿＿＿＿.

⑤ 그 책들은 나의 것이다.

　　The books are ＿＿＿＿＿＿.

⑥ 이 정원은 우리들의 것이다.

　　This garden is ＿＿＿＿＿＿.

정답 A의 정답은 앞 페이지의 오늘 공부했던 박스를 참고하세요. ① hers ② his ③ yours ④ theirs ⑤ mine ⑥ ours

be동사의 현재형

혼공개념 | be동사의 현재형이란?

1 be동사의 현재형: '~이다, ~있다'라는 의미로 쓰이는 동사

	인칭	인칭대명사	be동사
단수	1인칭	I	am
	2인칭	you	are
	3인칭	he / she	is
		it	
복수	1인칭	we	are
	2인칭	you	
	3인칭	they	

1) 사용: 주로 '주어(은, 는, 이, 가)' 다음에 쓰여서 주어에 대해 이야기할 때 쓰임

예 He + is handsome.　　He + is my superstar.
　　그는　잘생겼다　　　　그는　나의 슈퍼스타이다

He is in the building.
그 건물에 있다

혼공 팁

주어와 be동사를 줄여서 쓰는 것을 축약이라고 한다.

예 I am = I'm　　You are = You're　　He is = He's
　 It is = It's　　We are = We're　　They are = They're

2) 부정: be동사 + not을 써서 '~가 아니다, ~있지 않다'라고 표현하는 것

예 He is not handsome.　　He is not in the building.
　　　잘생긴 게 아니다　　　　　건물에 있지 않다

혼공 연습

A 다음 단어와 어울리는 be동사의 현재형을 쓰시오.

① I _____ you _____ he _____

② she _____ it _____ we _____

③ you _____ they _____ he _____

④ I _____ she _____ you _____

⑤ we _____ they _____ it _____

⑥ he _____ you _____ I _____

β 다음 빈칸을 적절한 be동사의 현재형으로 채우시오.

	인칭	인칭대명사	be동사
단수	1인칭	I	
	2인칭	you	
	3인칭	he / she	
		it	
복수	1인칭	we	
	2인칭	you	
	3인칭	they	

A 다음 우리말 의미를 참고하여 빈칸에 들어갈 영단어를 쓰시오.

① 나는 운이 좋다.   I _____ lucky.

② 하늘이 맑다.   The sky _____ clear.

③ 우리는 오랜 친구다.   We _____ old friends.

B 다음 우리말 의미와 같도록 단어들을 알맞게 배열하시오.

① Julian은 젊지 않다.

Julian / not / young / is   _____

② 그들은 화가 나 있다.

they / angry / are   _____

③ 나는 카페에 있다.

in the cafe / am / I   _____

C 다음 우리말로 된 자기소개서를 보고 빈칸에 알맞은 영어 표현을 쓰시오.

안녕하세요? 제 이름은 OOO 입니다. 제 아버지께서는 파일럿이십니다. 제 어머니
께서는 의사이십니다.

Hi, my name _____. My father _____.

_____.

A. 다음 빈칸을 예시처럼 채우시오.

	인칭	인칭대명사	be동사
단수	1인칭	I	am
	2인칭	you	
	3인칭	he / she	
		it	
복수	1인칭	we	
	2인칭	you	
	3인칭	they	

B. 다음 우리말을 보고 빈칸에 알맞은 be동사를 쓰시오.

① 나는 운이 좋다.　　　　I _____ lucky.

② 하늘이 맑다.　　　　　The sky _____ clear.

③ 우리는 오랜 친구다.　　We _____ old friends .

④ Julian은 젊지 않다.　　Julian _____ not young.

⑤ 그들은 화가 나 있다.　　They _____ angry.

⑥ 나는 카페에 있다.　　　I _____ in the cafe.

정답　A의 정답은 앞 페이지의 오늘 공부했던 박스를 참고하세요.　① am　② is　③ are　④ is　⑤ are　⑥ am

be동사의 과거형

 혼공개념 be동사의 과거형이란?

1 be동사의 과거형: was, were를 말하며 '~이었다(였다)', '~있었다' 라는 의미로 쓰임

  1) 사용: 주어가 단수이면 was, 복수이면 were를 사용

    예 Paul + was my classmate.

      They + were in my room.

  혼공 팁

  주어가 A and(그리고) B와 같이 쓰여도 하나가 아니기 때문에 복수로 취급한다.

  예 Eddie and Jason were friends.

  2) 부정: was, were 다음에 not을 써서 '~아니었다, ~있지 않았다'라고 표현하는 것

    예 Paul was not my classmate.

      They were not in my room.

	인칭	인칭대명사	be동사의 현재형	be동사의 과거형
단수	1인칭	I	am	was
	2인칭	you	are	were
	3인칭	he / she	is	was
		it		
복수	1인칭	we	are	were
	2인칭	you		
	3인칭	they		

혼공 연습

A 다음 단어와 어울리는 be동사의 과거형을 쓰시오.

① I _____ you _____ he _____

② she _____ it _____ we _____

③ you _____ they _____ he _____

④ I _____ she _____ you _____

⑤ we _____ they _____ it _____

⑥ he _____ you _____ I _____

β 다음 빈칸을 적절한 be동사로 채우시오.

	인칭	인칭대명사	be동사의 현재형	be동사의 과거형
단수	1인칭	I		
	2인칭	you		
	3인칭	he / she		
		it		
복수	1인칭	we		
	2인칭	you		
	3인칭	they		

A 다음 우리말 의미를 참고하여 빈칸에 들어갈 영단어를 쓰시오.

① 이것은 <u>그녀의 것이었다.</u>　　　　 This _____ _____.

② Kevin은 <u>의사였었다.</u>　　　　　 Kevin _____ a _____.

③ Robin은 <u>그의 방 안에 있지 않았다.</u>　 Robin _____ _____ in his room.

④ 그들은 <u>피곤하지 않았다.</u>　　　　 They _____ _____ tired.

B 다음 주어진 말들을 의미에 맞게 배열하시오.

① my English teacher / Mr. Park / was

_____

② in the office / Mr. Smith / was

_____

③ in Korea / Andy and his parents / were

_____

C Daniel과 Olivia가 작년에 좋아했던 과목을 참고하여 빈칸을 채우시오.

	Daniel	Olivia
Last year	P.E., painting	English, music

Last year, English and music _____ Olivia's favorite subjects.

_____ and _____ _____ Daniel's favorite subjects.

A. 다음 빈칸을 예시처럼 채우시오.

	인칭	인칭대명사	be동사의 현재형	be동사의 과거형
단수	1인칭	I	am	was
	2인칭	you		
	3인칭	he / she		
		it		
복수	1인칭	we		
	2인칭	you		
	3인칭	they		

B. 다음 우리말을 보고 빈칸에 알맞은 단어를 쓰시오.

① 이것은 <u>그녀의 것이었다.</u>　　　　　This _____ _____.

② Robin은 <u>그의 방 안에 있지 않았다.</u>　　Robin _____ _____ in his room.

C. 빈칸을 was 또는 were로 채우고, 문장 해석을 적으시오.

③ Mr. Park _____ my English teacher.

_____

④ Mr. Smith _____ in the office.

_____

⑤ Andy and his parents _____ in Korea.

_____

be동사의 의문문

1 be동사의 의문문: 주어(은, 는, 이, 가)와 be동사의 자리를 바꾸어 질문을 하는 문장

평서문(보통문장)		의문문
<u>He</u> <u>is</u> your dad.	⇒	<u>Is</u> <u>he</u> your dad?
<u>Alex</u> <u>was</u> her best friend.	⇒	<u>Was</u> <u>Alex</u> her best friend?
<u>They</u> <u>are</u> sick.	⇒	<u>Are</u> <u>they</u> sick?
<u>The boys</u> <u>were</u> happy.	⇒	<u>Were</u> <u>the boys</u> happy?

2 대답하기: Yes(긍정), No(부정)을 활용

[예] Is he your dad?

긍정　Yes, he is (my dad).　　　부정　No, he is not (my dad).

No, he isn't (my dad).

[예] Was Alex her best friend?

긍정　Yes, he was (her best friend).　부정　No, he was not (her best friend).

No, he wasn't (her best friend).

[예] Are they sick?

긍정　Yes, they are (sick).　　　부정　No, they are not (sick).

No, they aren't (sick).

혼공 연습

A 다음 문장을 의문문으로 바꾸시오.

① He is your dad. → _____?

② Alex was her best friend. → _____?

③ They are sick. → _____?

④ The boys were happy. → _____?

B 다음 질문에 대해 긍정과 부정의 대답을 하시오.

① Is he your dad?

긍정: _____, 부정: _____

② Was Alex her best friend?

긍정: _____, 부정: _____

③ Are they sick?

긍정: _____, 부정: _____

④ Were the boys happy?

긍정: _____, 부정: _____

A 다음 우리말 의미와 같도록 단어들을 알맞게 배열하시오.

① 그녀는 의사니?

a doctor / she / is _____

② 너 피곤하니?

tired / you / are _____

③ 그들은 늦었니?

they / were / late _____

④ 그녀는 네 누나니?

she / your / sister / is _____

B 다음 Kate와 Michael의 모습을 나타낸 사진을 보고 질문에 알맞은 응답을 하시오.

① A: Is Kate a nurse?

   B: _____

② A: Is Michael a farmer?

   B: _____

A. 다음 문장을 의문문으로 바꾸시오.

① He is your dad.   _____?

② Alex was her best friend.   _____?

③ They are sick.   _____?

④ The boys were happy.   _____?

B. 다음 우리말을 보고 빈칸에 알맞은 영어 단어를 쓰시오.

⑤ 그녀는 의사니?   _____ _____ a doctor?

　　네, 그녀는 의사에요.   _____, _____ _____.

⑥ 너 피곤하니?   _____ _____ tired?

　　네, 저는 피곤해요.   _____, I _____.

⑦ 그들은 늦었니?   _____ they _____?

　　아니요, 그들은 늦지 않았어요. _____, _____ _____ _____.

⑧ 그녀는 네 누나니?   _____ _____ your _____?

　　아니요, 그녀는 내 누나가 아니에요. _____, _____ is _____.

정답 ① Is he your dad ② Was Alex her best friend ③ Are they sick ④ Were the boys happy ⑤ Is, she, Yes, she, is ⑥ Are, you, Yes, am ⑦ Were, late, No, they, were, not ⑧ Is, she, sister, No, she, not

지시대명사 / 지시형용사

🔍 혼공개념 지시대명사란?

단수	복수	의미
this 이것 (이 사람)	these 이것들 (이 사람들)	가까이 있는 사람이나 사물
that 저것 (저 사람)	those 저것들 (저 사람들)	조금 떨어져 있는 사람이나 사물

[예] <u>This</u> is a peach.   <u>That</u> is a store.
　　이것　　　　　　　　　　저것

<u>These</u> are his dogs.   <u>Those</u> are my friends.
이것들　　　　　　　　　　저 사람들

혼공 팁

의문문을 만들 때는 주어와 동사의 순서를 바꾸면 된다.

<u>Is this</u> a peach?   <u>Is that</u> a store?

<u>Are these</u> his dogs?   <u>Are those</u> my friends?

🔍 혼공개념 지시형용사란?

의미	
this 이 + 단수명사	these 이 + 복수명사
that 저 + 단수명사	those 저 + 복수명사

[예] <u>This(that) + chair</u> is mine.   Is <u>this(that) chair</u> mine?
　　이(저) + 의자(단수)　　　　　　　　이(저) + 의자(단수)

<u>These(those) + students</u> are from Spain.
　　이(저) + 학생들(복수)

Are <u>these(those) students</u> from Spain?
　　이(저) 학생들(복수)

A 다음 우리말을 보고 알맞은 영단어를 빈칸에 쓰시오.

① 이것(사람) _____ 저것(사람) _____

② 이것(사람)들 _____ 저것(사람)들 _____

③ 이 의자 _____ _____

④ 저 학생들 _____ _____

B 다음 우리말 의미를 보고 빈칸에 알맞은 영단어를 쓰시오.

① 이 분(사람)은 나의 어머니이시다.   ② 저 사람들은 내 친구들이다.

_____ is my mother.   _____ are my friends.

③ 이 의자는 내 것이다.   ④ 저 학생들은 스페인 출신이다.

_____ _____ is mine.   _____ _____ are from Spain.

C 다음 문장을 의문문으로 바꾸어 쓰시오.

① This is a peach.   →   _____

② These are his dogs.   →   _____

③ That chair is mine.   →   _____

④ These students are from Spain. →   _____

A 다음 사진을 보고 괄호 안에서 알맞은 단어를 고르시오.

① (This / That) is my house.

② (These / Those) are my sisters.

B 다음 괄호 안에서 알맞은 단어를 고르시오.

① (This / These) are students from Australia.

② (This / These) shoes are expensive.

③ (That / Those) is his new car.

④ (That / Those) letters are not yours.

C 다음 우리말 의미와 같도록 단어들을 알맞게 배열하시오.

① 이 사람은 내 형이다. (brother / this / my / is)

_____

② 이 학생들은 내 학급 친구들이다. (my / these / students / classmates / are)

_____

③ 서울은 큰 도시니? (a / big / Seoul / city / is)

_____

A. 다음 단어들을 보고 ①번의 예시처럼 빈칸을 채우시오.

		우리말 의미
①	this	이것, 이 사람, 이
②	that	
③	these	
④	those	
⑤	this chair	
⑥	those letters	
⑦	these shoes	

B. 다음 빈칸을 주어진 우리말 의미에 맞게 채우시오.

⑧ 이 사람은 내 형이다.

_____ is my _____.

⑨ 저것은 내 집이다.

_____ is my _____.

⑩ 이 신발은 비싸다.

_____ shoes _____ _____.

⑪ 이 학생들은 내 학급 친구들이다.

_____ _____ are my _____.

⑫ 저 편지들은 네 것이 아니다.

_____ _____ are not _____.

정답 ② 저것, 저 사람, 저 ③ 이것들, 이 사람들, 이 ④ 저것들, 저 사람들, 저 ⑤ 이 의자 ⑥ 저 편지들 ⑦ 이 신발(들) ⑧ This, brother ⑨ That, house ⑩ These, are, expensive ⑪ These, students, classmates ⑫ Those, letters, yours

일반동사의 현재형 1

🔔 혼공개념 일반동사란?

1 일반동사: be동사 외에 동작이나 상태를 나타내는 동사

　　[예] play, study, like, go...

2 현재형의 쓰임

　　1) 현재의 동작, 상태, 감정을 표현

　　　[예] I <u>feel</u> happy.

　　2) 반복되는 일상의 습관을 나타냄

　　　[예] I <u>get up</u> early in the morning.　　Tom <u>begins</u> work at 9:00.

　　3) 불변의 진리나 일반적 사실을 나타냄

　　　[예] One and one <u>makes</u> two.　　The sun <u>rises</u> in the east.

혼공 팁

주어가 3인칭 단수일 때에는 동사 뒤에 s, es를 붙인다.

[예] · She work<u>s</u> at a bank.　· Kevin watch<u>es</u> TV.

　　· Jack and Jill like each other. (주어 3인칭 복수)

🔔 혼공개념 주어가 3인칭 단수일 때 일반동사의 현재형 만들기

1 동사가 s, ch, sh로 끝날 때 + es

　　[예] pass ⇒ passes,　finish ⇒ finishes,　watch ⇒ watches

2 동사가 자음 + y로 끝날 때 ⇒ y를 i로 바꾸고 + es

　　[예] study ⇒ studies,　try ⇒ tries　　　　[주의] play ⇒ plays,　enjoy ⇒ enjoys

3 기타

　　[예] go ⇒ goes,　do ⇒ does,　have ⇒ has

혼공 연습

A 다음 문장을 읽고, 밑줄 친 주어가 3인칭 단수이면 O, 그렇지 않으면 X 표시를 하시오.

① <u>I</u> feel happy. (   )

② <u>Tom</u> begins work at 9:00. (   )

③ <u>The sun</u> rises in the east. (   )

④ <u>She</u> works at a bank. (   )

⑤ <u>Kevin</u> watches TV. (   )

⑥ <u>Jack and Jill</u> like each other. (   )

β 주어가 3인칭 단수일 때 다음 동사들의 현재형을 쓰시오.

① begin _____	feel _____	get _____
② make _____	rise _____	study _____
③ pass _____	try _____	go _____
④ watch _____	do _____	have _____
⑤ finish _____	study _____	play _____
⑥ enjoy _____	go _____	watch _____
⑦ do _____	pass _____	finish _____

A 다음 우리말을 보고 빈칸에 알맞은 영단어를 쓰시오.

① 민수는 라디오를 듣는다.

Minsu _____ to the radio.

② 내 할아버지께서 신문을 읽으신다.

My grandfather _____ the newspaper.

③ 내 동생이 그의 방을 청소한다.

My brother _____ _____ room.

④ Jason은 양치를 하루에 세 번 한다.

Jason _____ his teeth three times a day.

⑤ Tom은 매일 아침 우유를 마신다.

Tom _____ milk every morning.

B 다음 괄호 안에서 알맞은 단어를 선택하시오.

① (They / Kevin) waters the garden in the evening.

② (My uncle / My parents) fixes the car.

③ (Mary / I) have a computer.

C 다음 우리말로 된 일정을 참고하여 빈칸을 적절한 영단어로 채우시오.

그녀는 월요일에 영어를 공부합니다. 화요일에 그녀는 라디오를 듣습니다.
수요일에 그녀는 테니스를 합니다. 목요일에 그녀는 기타를 연주합니다.

She _____ English on Monday. On Tuesday she _____ to the radio. On
Wednesday she _____ tennis. On Thursday she _____ the guitar.

A. 다음 단어들을 보고 ①번의 예시처럼 빈칸을 채우시오.

	단어	주어가 3인칭 단수일 때의 현재형
①	begin	begins
②	feel	
③	get	
④	make	
⑤	rise	
⑥	study	
⑦	pass	
⑧	try	
⑨	go	
⑩	watch	
⑪	do	
⑫	have	
⑬	finish	
⑭	play	
⑮	enjoy	
⑯	listen	
⑰	read	
⑱	clean	
⑲	drink	
⑳	water	
㉑	fix	
㉒	brush	

정답 ② feels ③ gets ④ makes ⑤ rises ⑥ studies ⑦ passes ⑧ tries ⑨ goes ⑩ watches ⑪ does ⑫ has ⑬ finishes ⑭ plays
⑮ enjoys ⑯ listens ⑰ reads ⑱ cleans ⑲ drinks ⑳ waters ㉑ fixes ㉒ brushes

일반동사의 현재형 2

 혼공개념 일반동사의 부정이란?

1 일반동사의 부정

1) 대부분의 경우: do not / don't + 일반동사의 원형(s, es 안 붙은 현재형)

[예] I don't like mango juice.

Please do not eat or drink here.

2) 주어가 3인칭 단수: does not / doesn't + 일반동사의 원형

[예] Jessica doesn't like Mexican food.

 혼공개념 일반동사의 현재 진행형이란?

1 현재 진행형의 의미: ~하고 있는 중이다

1) 현재 진행형 만들기: be동사(am, is, are) + 동사 ~ing

[예] I am listening to the noise.

My dad is watering the garden.

My cousins are baking cookies.

It is snowing outside.

2) 현재 진행형 부정하기: be동사(am, is, are) + not + 동사 ~ing

[예] I am not listening to the noise.

My dad is not watering the garden.

My cousins are not baking cookies.

It is not snowing outside.

A 다음 문장을 don't 또는 doesn't를 사용해서 부정하시오.

① I like mango juice.　　　　　_____

② Please eat or drink here.　_____

③ Jessica likes Mexican food.　_____

④ She drinks coffee.　　　　　_____

⑤ They like music.　　　　　　_____

β 다음 문장을 현재 진행형을 사용하여 다시 쓰시오.

① My cousins bake cookies.　_____

② My dad waters the garden.　_____

③ I listen to the noise.　　　　_____

④ It snows outside.　　　　　　_____

C B에서 만든 현재 진행형을 not으로 부정하시오.

① _____

② _____

③ _____

④ _____

A 다음 괄호 안에서 알맞은 것을 선택하시오.

① Mike (don't / doesn't) worry about it.

② Melanie (don't / doesn't) enjoy her work.

③ Tom and Matthew (don't / doesn't) do yoga on Sundays.

B 다음 우리말을 보고 빈칸에 알맞은 영단어를 쓰시오.

① 나는 만화책을 읽고 있는 중이다.

I am _____ a comic book.

② 나의 부모님들께서는 그들의 방에서 주무시는 중이다.

My parents _____ _____ in their room.

③ 아기는 거실에서 울고 있는 중이다.

The baby _____ _____ in the living room.

C John이 다음과 같이 물었을 때 <보기>의 표현들을 참고하여 3가지의 대답을 만드시오.

John: Hey, what are you doing?

<보기>	study science	fix my bicycle	play baseball

① I am _____.

② I _____.

③ _____.

A. 다음 문장들을 보고 ①번의 예시처럼 부정하시오.

① I like mango juice.　　　I don't like mango juice.

② Jessica likes Mexican food. _____

③ She drinks coffee. _____

④ They like music. _____

B. 다음 빈칸을 주어진 우리말 의미에 맞게 채우시오.

⑤ 나는 과학을 공부하고 있는 중이다.

I _____ _____ _____.

⑥ 나는 내 자전거를 고치고 있는 중이다.

I _____ _____ _____ _____.

⑦ 나는 야구하는 중이다.

I _____ _____ _____.

정답 ② Jessica doesn't like Mexican food.　③ She doesn't drink coffee.　④ They don't like music.　⑤ am studying science　⑥ am fixing my bicycle ⑦ am playing baseball

일반동사의 과거형 1

1 일반동사의 과거형

1) 의미: 현재보다 이전에 일어났던 일을 표현함

2) 형태: 대부분의 경우 '동사원형 + ed'

  예 watch(보다) - watch<u>ed</u>(보았다)

혼공 팁

주어가 3인칭 단수라고 해도 일반동사의 과거형에는 s, es를 붙이지 않는다.
예 She watch<u>ed</u> TV. (O)

3) 일반동사의 규칙 과거형 만들기

원리	예시
동사의 원형 + ed	listen - listened / look - looked / rain - rained / watch - watched / finish - finished
-e로 끝나는 동사 + d	love - loved / live - lived / hate - hated / close - closed / like - liked / dance - danced
자음 + y로 끝나는 동사 → y를 i로 바꾸고 + ed	try - tried / cry - cried / study - studied
단모음 + 단자음으로 끝나는 1음절 동사 → 마지막 자음 한번 더 쓰고 + ed	stop - stopped / drop - dropped

혼공 팁

현재와 과거형의 형태가 동일한 동사들도 있다.
예 cut, put, hurt, read...

A 다음 동사의 과거형을 두 번씩 적으시오.

① listen _____ _____

② look _____ _____

③ rain _____ _____

④ watch _____ _____

⑤ finish _____ _____

⑥ love _____ _____

⑦ live _____ _____

⑧ hate _____ _____

⑨ close _____ _____

⑩ like _____ _____

⑪ dance _____ _____

⑫ try _____ _____

⑬ cry _____ _____

⑭ study _____ _____

⑮ stop _____ _____

⑯ drop _____ _____

⑰ play _____ _____

A 다음 문장에 들어갈 알맞은 단어를 <보기>에서 골라 쓰시오.

<보기>	invited	washed	helped	brushed	played

① She ＿＿＿＿＿＿ the dishes.

② I ＿＿＿＿＿＿ her to my house.

③ Yuri ＿＿＿＿＿＿ her teeth.

④ I ＿＿＿＿＿＿ baseball yesterday.

B 다음 우리말과 일치하도록 괄호 안의 표현을 참고하여 영작하시오.

① 그들은 춤을 추었다. (dance)

＿＿＿＿＿＿＿＿＿＿＿＿＿＿＿＿＿＿＿＿

② 그는 문을 닫았다. (close the door)

＿＿＿＿＿＿＿＿＿＿＿＿＿＿＿＿＿＿＿＿

③ 그들은 시험에 대비하여 열심히 공부했다. (study hard for the test)

＿＿＿＿＿＿＿＿＿＿＿＿＿＿＿＿＿＿＿＿

C 다음 단어들 중 동사를 과거형으로 바꾼 뒤 의미에 맞게 나열하시오.

① (a surprise party / we / plan) ＿＿＿＿＿＿＿＿＿＿＿＿＿＿＿＿＿

② (sing / a song / I) ＿＿＿＿＿＿＿＿＿＿＿＿＿＿＿＿＿

A. 다음 단어들을 보고 ①번의 예시처럼 빈칸을 채우시오.

	단어	과거형
①	listen	listened
②	look	
③	rain	
④	watch	
⑤	finish	
⑥	love	
⑦	live	
⑧	hate	
⑨	close	
⑩	like	
⑪	dance	
⑫	try	
⑬	cry	
⑭	study	
⑮	stop	
⑯	drop	
⑰	brush	
⑱	play	
⑲	wash	
⑳	invite	
㉑	plan	
㉒	sing	
㉓	put	
㉔	cut	

정답 ② looked ③ rained ④ watched ⑤ finished ⑥ loved ⑦ lived ⑧ hated ⑨ closed ⑩ liked ⑪ danced ⑫ tried ⑬ cried ⑭ studied
⑮ stopped ⑯ dropped ⑰ brushed ⑱ played ⑲ washed ⑳ invited ㉑ planned ㉒ sang ㉓ put ㉔ cut

13

일반동사의 과거형 2

 혼공개념 | 일반동사의 불규칙 과거형이란?

1 일반동사의 불규칙 과거형: 동사원형 + 'ed, d'가 아닌 다른 형태를 띄는 경우

	원형	과거형		원형	과거형
1	begin	began	21	break	broke
2	bring	brought	22	buy	bought
3	catch	caught	23	choose	chose
4	come	came	24	do	did
5	draw	drew	25	eat	ate
6	feel	felt	26	find	found
7	forget	forgot	27	get	got
8	give	gave	28	go	went
9	grow	grew	29	have	had
10	hear	heard	30	know	knew
11	lose	lost	31	leave	left
12	make	made	32	meet	met
13	run	ran	33	ride	rode
14	say	said	34	see	saw
15	send	sent	35	sing	sang
16	sleep	slept	36	speak	spoke
17	stand	stood	37	swim	swam
18	take	took	38	teach	taught
19	tell	told	39	win	won
20	write	wrote	40	wear	wore

다음 동사의 과거형을 적으시오. (한 단어 당 두 번씩)

	원형	과거형			원형	과거형	
1	begin			21	break		
2	bring			22	buy		
3	catch			23	choose		
4	come			24	do		
5	draw			25	eat		
6	feel			26	find		
7	forget			27	get		
8	give			28	go		
9	grow			29	have		
10	hear			30	know		
11	lose			31	leave		
12	make			32	meet		
13	run			33	ride		
14	say			34	see		
15	send			35	sing		
16	sleep			36	speak		
17	stand			37	swim		
18	take			38	teach		
19	tell			39	win		
20	write			40	wear		

A 다음 빈칸에 주어진 동사의 과거형을 쓰시오.

① I _____ lunch with Jane. (have)

② Jun _____ a book in the library. (read)

③ I _____ my dad's birthday. (forget)

④ Alex _____ his wallet at the airport. (lose)

B 다음 괄호 안에 주어진 동사의 알맞은 형태를 빈칸에 쓰시오.

① They (take) many pictures last night. _____

② I (break) my arm last year. _____

③ She (come) back from Russia last year. _____

C 다음은 Chloe가 자기 전에 쓴 일기이다. 밑줄 친 단어를 알맞은 형태로 고치시오.

> I get up early in the morning and I study English. At noon, I have lunch
> with my parents. My mom makes bulgogi for me. I enjoy it.

⇓

> I _____ up early in the morning and I _____ English. At noon, I _____
> lunch with my parents. My mom _____ bulgogi for me. I _____ it.

A. 다음 단어들을 보고 ①번의 예시처럼 빈칸을 채우시오.

	원형	과거형		원형	과거형
①	begin	began	㉑	break	
②	bring		㉒	buy	
③	catch		㉓	choose	
④	come		㉔	do	
⑤	draw		㉕	eat	
⑥	feel		㉖	find	
⑦	forget		㉗	get	
⑧	give		㉘	go	
⑨	grow		㉙	have	
⑩	hear		㉚	know	
⑪	lose		㉛	leave	
⑫	make		㉜	meet	
⑬	run		㉝	ride	
⑭	say		㉞	see	
⑮	send		㉟	sing	
⑯	sleep		㊱	speak	
⑰	stand		㊲	swim	
⑱	take		㊳	teach	
⑲	tell		㊴	win	
⑳	write		㊵	wear	

정답 이전 페이지를 넘겨 박스 속의 단어를 참고하세요.

일반동사의 과거형 3

혼공개념

혼공개념 일반동사 과거의 부정이란?

1 일반동사의 과거 부정: did not / didn't + 일반동사의 원형

> [예] I didn't work at the post office.　　　She didn't study hard.
>
> 　　 Michael didn't use chopsticks.　　　He didn't like the restaurant.

혼공 팁

주어가 3인칭 단수라 하더라도 did not, didn't 뒤에 오는 동사에는 s, es를 붙이지 않는다.
[예] She didn't studies hard. (X)

혼공개념 과거 진행형이란?

1 과거 진행형의 의미: ~하고 있는 중이었다

1) 과거 진행형 만들기: be동사(was, were) + 동사 ~ing

> [예] I was listening to the noise.
>
> 　　 My dad was watering the garden.
>
> 　　 My cousins were baking cookies.
>
> 　　 It was snowing outside.

2) 과거 진행형 부정하기: be동사(was, were) + not + 동사 ~ing

> [예] I was not listening to the noise.
>
> 　　 My dad was not watering the garden.
>
> 　　 My cousins were not baking cookies.
>
> 　　 It was not snowing outside.

A 다음 문장을 didn't 또는 did not을 사용해서 부정하시오.

① I worked at the post office.

_____

② She studied hard.

_____

③ Michael used chopsticks.

_____

④ He liked the restaurant.

_____

β 주어진 동사를 사용해서 <보기>와 같이 과거 진행형으로 만드시오.

<보기>	make (I)	⇒	I was making

① play (they)　　　　　　　→ _____

② use (I)　　　　　　　　→ _____

③ rain (it)　　　　　　　→ _____

④ listen (we)　　　　　　→ _____

⑤ water (I)　　　　　　　→ _____

⑥ study (the students)　　→ _____

⑦ make (my mom)　　　　→ _____

A 주어진 문장을 아래와 같이 부정문으로 만드시오.

He took tennis lessons. → He didn't take tennis lessons.

① Jason went to the hospital.　　→ _____

② You put my wallet on the desk.　→ _____

③ We ate pasta for lunch.　　　　→ _____

④ They visited the shopping mall.

　　→ _____

B 우리말과 주어진 표현을 활용하여 영작하시오.

① 그는 그 영화를 즐기지 않았다. (enjoy / the movie)

　　_____

② 그녀는 두통이 있지 않았다. (have a headache)

　　_____

③ 그는 브라질에서 살지 않았다. (live / in Brazil)

　　_____

C Eddie가 다음과 같이 물었을 때 대답을 2개 쓰시오.

Eddie: Hey, what were you doing?

나 : Hmm...　　I _____

　　　　　　　　I _____

A. 다음 단어들을 보고 ①번의 예시처럼 부정문을 만드시오.

① I worked at the post office.　　I didn't work at the post office.

② She studied hard.　　_____

③ Michael used chopsticks.　　_____

④ He liked the restaurant.　　_____

⑤ Jason went to the hospital.　　_____

⑥ We ate pasta for lunch.　　_____

B. 다음을 ⑦번과 같이 과거 진행형으로 바꾸시오.

⑦ They play　　They were playing.

⑧ I use　　_____

⑨ It rains　　_____

⑩ We listen　　_____

⑪ I water　　_____

⑫ The students study　　_____

⑬ My mom makes　　_____

정답 ② She didn't study hard. ③ Michael didn't use chopsticks. ④ He didn't like the restaurant. ⑤ Jason didn't go to the hospital. ⑥ We didn't eat pasta for lunch. ⑧ I was using ⑨ It was raining ⑩ We were listening ⑪ I was watering ⑫ The students were studying ⑬ My mom was making

일반동사의 의문문

일반동사의 의문문이란?

1 일반동사의 의문문: Do, Does, Did + 주어(은, 는, 이, 가) ~?

예 You speak English. ⇒ Do you speak English?

Jihoo speaks English. ⇒ Does Jihoo speak English?

She spoke English. ⇒ Did she speak English?

혼공 팁

앞에 Do, Does, Did 중 어떤 것이 오더라도 주어 다음에는 동사의 원형을 써야 한다.

예 Does Jihoo <u>speak</u> English?   Did she <u>speak</u> English?

2 대답하기: Yes(긍정), No(부정)을 활용

예 Do you speak English?

긍정 Yes, I do.

부정 No, I don't.

Does Jihoo speak English?

긍정 Yes, he does.

부정 No, he doesn't.

Did she speak English?

긍정 Yes, she did.

부정 No, she didn't.

A 다음 문장을 의문문으로 바꾸시오.

① You speak English. → _____

② Jihoo speaks English. → _____

③ She spoke English. → _____

④ You finished your work. → _____

⑤ Mr. Kim painted this picture. → _____

⑥ Jane wrote this book. → _____

⑦ He takes a shower every day. → _____

β A에서 만든 의문문 중 두 개를 선택하여 긍정과 부정의 대답을 하시오.

① _____

긍정: _____, 부정: _____

② _____

긍정: _____, 부정: _____

A 다음 괄호 안의 단어를 알맞은 형태로 고치시오.

① Did you (liked) his idea? _____

② Does he (eats) tomatoes? _____

③ Does she (lives) in an apartment? _____

④ Did she (brought) an umbrella? _____

β <보기>처럼 주어진 문장을 의문문으로 만든 뒤, 긍정 또는 부정의 대답을 하시오.

<보기> They lived in Canada last year. (긍정)

→ Did they live in Canada last year?

Yes, they did.

① His family visited Ghana. (긍정)

→ _____ _____

② You slept well last night. (부정)

→ _____ _____

③ She went to his birthday party. (긍정)

→ _____ _____

④ You took a shower after the soccer match. (부정)

→ _____ _____

A. 다음 문장을 보고 ①의 예시처럼 의문문을 만드시오.

① You speak English.　　　　→ Do you speak English?

② Jihoo speaks English.　　　→ _____

③ She spoke English.　　　　→ _____

④ You finished your work.　　→ _____

⑤ Mr. Kim painted this picture.　→ _____

⑥ Jane wrote this book.　　　→ _____

⑦ He takes a shower every day.　→ _____

B. 다음 문장을 보고 ⑧의 예시처럼 알맞은 대답을 하시오.

⑧ Did you like his idea?

　　　　　　긍정: _____Yes, I did._____

⑨ Does he eat tomatoes?

　　　　　　부정: _____

⑩ Does she drink soda?

　　　　　　부정: _____

⑪ Did you bring an umbrella?

　　　　　　긍정: _____

정답 ② Does Jihoo speak English? ③ Did she speak English? ④ Did you finish your work? ⑤ Did Mr. Kim paint this picture? ⑥ Did Jane write this book? ⑦ Does he take a shower every day? ⑨ No, he doesn't. ⑩ No, she doesn't. ⑪ Yes, I did.

16

부정관사 / 정관사

혼공개념 부정관사(a, an)란?

1 부정관사: 세상에 많은 것들 중 '하나, 하나의'라는 의미로 셀 수 있는 명사 앞에
a 또는 an으로 쓰임

[예] a car, a school, a book, a desk, an apple

1) a를 붙이는 경우: 명사가 자음으로 시작할 때

[예] a car, a school, a book, a horse...

2) an을 붙이는 경우: 명사가 모음으로 시작할 때

[예] an apple, an hour, an egg, an orange...

혼공개념 정관사(the)란?

1 정관사: 주로 '그'라는 의미로 명사 앞에서 쓰임

1) 앞에서 한번 언급된 것을 다시 말할 때 씀

[예] There was a dog. The dog was BINGO.

2) 대화하는 사람들이 서로 알고 있는 대상을 가리킬 때 씀

[예] Kevin is in the kitchen.

3) 지구, 태양과 같이 유일한 대상을 가리킬 때 씀

[예] The Earth moves around the Sun.

A 다음 명사 앞에 a, an 중 적절한 것을 선택해서 <보기>와 같이 쓰시오.

<보기>	boat	___a boat___

① car _____   school _____

② apple _____   desk _____

③ book _____   orange _____

④ computer _____   egg _____

⑤ hour _____   horse _____

β 다음 우리말을 보고 빈칸에 들어갈 알맞은 영단어를 쓰시오.

① 그 개는 빙고였다.

_____ _____ was BINGO.

② Kevin은 그 부엌에 있었다.

Kevin was in _____ _____.

③ 지구는 태양 주위를 움직인다.

_____ _____ moves around _____ _____.

A 다음 빈칸에 a, an 중 알맞은 것을 쓰시오.

① _____ apartment   _____ snake   _____ fox

② _____ iron   _____ owl   _____ airplane

③ _____ ice cream   _____ university   _____ daughter

B 다음 밑줄 친 부분을 문법적으로 바르게 고치시오.

① My mom is <u>an nurse</u>.   _____

② These are <u>a ducks</u>.   _____

③ It is <u>a expensive</u> car.   _____

C 다음 빈칸에 a, an, the 중 알맞은 것을 하나 쓰시오.

① My place is on _____ second floor.

② There is _____ airplane in _____ sky.

③ _____ Earth goes around _____ Sun.

④ Jun saw students and _____ students were tall.

⑤ I met three boys and _____ boys were kind.

⑥ A: Where is Melanie?   B: Oh, she is in _____ living room.

A. 다음 단어들을 보고 ①의 예시처럼 a, an 중 적절한 것으로 빈칸을 채우시오.

①	a	boat
②		car
③		apple
④		school
⑤		desk
⑥		book
⑦		orange
⑧		computer
⑨		egg
⑩		hour
⑪		horse
⑫		snake
⑬		fox
⑭		daughter
⑮		owl
⑯		airplane
⑰		ice cream
⑱		university
⑲		iron
⑳		apartment

정답 ② a ③ an ④ a ⑤ a ⑥ a ⑦ an ⑧ a ⑨ an ⑩ an ⑪ a ⑫ a ⑬ a ⑭ a ⑮ an ⑯ an ⑰ an ⑱ a ⑲ an ⑳ an

17

의문사 의문문

혼공개념 의문사란?

1 의문사: 상대방에게 질문을 할 때 쓰는 who, what, when, where, why, how

1) be동사일 때: 의문사 + be동사 + 주어 ?

You are who.   ⇒   Who are you?
당신은 누구이다.   당신은 누구세요?

[예] Why were you late?

Who was his math teacher?

2) 일반동사일 때: 의문사 + do / does / did + 주어 + 동사원형 ?

You live where.   ⇒   Where do you live?
당신은 어디에 산다.   당신은 어디에 사세요?

[예] What does he do?   Why did you like it?

When do you go to school?

3) 덩어리 표현: '의문사 + 형용사(부사, 명사)'가 하나의 의미를 이루어 의문문에 쓰임

[예] How old are you?   How much is it?

How long is it?   What time do you get up?

4) which, whose의 쓰임: which는 선택(어느 것), whose는 소유(누구의)를 물어봄

[예] Which is yours?   Which bag is yours?

Whose umbrella is this?

다음 단어들을 배열하여 의문사 의문문으로 만들고 우리말 해석을 쓰시오.

① you / who / are   _____?

　　　　　의미: _____?

② do / where / live / you   _____?

　　　　　의미: _____?

③ what / he / do / does   _____?

　　　　　의미: _____?

④ do / go / to school / when / you _____?

　　　　　의미: _____?

⑤ were / why / late / you   _____?

　　　　　의미: _____?

⑥ was / his / who / math teacher   _____?

　　　　　의미: _____?

⑦ did / why / it / like / you   _____?

　　　　　의미: _____?

우리말 의미에 맞게 알맞은 단어를 고르시오.

① 오늘은 무슨 요일이에요?

(How / What) day is it today?

② 오늘은 날씨가 어떤가요?

(How / Which) is the weather today?

③ 콘서트는 언제 시작하나요?

(How long / When) does the concert start?

B 다음 대화의 빈칸에 알맞은 의문사를 쓰시오.

① A: _____ computer is this?

B: It's John's.

② A: _____ time do you go to school?

B: 9 o'clock.

③ A: _____ tall are you?

B: I'm 170cm tall.

④ A: _____ did you have for breakfast?

B: I had cereal.

⑤ A: _____ _____ is the river?

B: It's about 50km long.

A. 다음 빈칸을 ①처럼 주어진 우리말 의미에 맞게 채우시오.

① 이 컴퓨터는 누구의 것이니?　　　　Whose computer is this?

② 너는 몇 시에 학교에 가니?　　　　_____ _____ do you go to school?

③ 너는 키가 얼마니?　　　　_____ _____ are you?

④ 너는 아침으로 무엇을 먹었니?　　　　_____ _____ you have for breakfast?

⑤ 그 강은 얼마나 기니?　　　　_____ _____ is the river?

B. 다음 우리말을 보고 ⑥처럼 영작하시오.

⑥ 당신은 누구세요?　　　　Who are you ?

⑦ 당신은 어디에 사세요?　　　　_____?

⑧ 그는 무엇을 하나요? (직업묻기)　　　　_____?

⑨ 당신은 언제 학교에 가나요?　　　　_____?

⑩ 당신은 왜 늦었어요?　　　　_____?

⑪ 누가 그의 선생님이었나요?　　　　_____?

⑫ 당신은 그것을 왜 좋아했나요?　　　　_____?

정답　② What, time　③ How, tall　④ What, did　⑤ How, long　⑦ Where do you live　⑧ What does he do　⑨ When do you go to school
⑩ Why were you late　⑪ Who was his teacher　⑫ Why did you like it

부가의문문

1 부가의문문: 말을 한 다음, 그 뒤에 상대방의 동의를 구하거나 확인을 위해 짧게 다시 질문을 하는 것

〔예〕 You are hungry, <u>aren't you</u>?

1) 부가의문문 만들기: 앞의 문장이 긍정이면 부정, 부정이면 긍정으로 만들되 앞에 나온 동사와 같은 시제를 사용함

〔예〕 You <u>were</u> happy. + <u>weren't</u> you?

⇒ You were happy, weren't you?

She <u>wasn't</u> sick. + <u>was</u> she?

⇒ She wasn't sick, was she?

2) 부가의문문에 대답하기: 우리말 해석과 관계없이 긍정이면 Yes, 부정이면 No로 함

You liked it, didn't you?	You didn't like it, did you?
긍정: 좋아했다 ⇒ Yes, I did.	
부정: 좋아하지 않았다 ⇒ No, I didn't.	

3) 명령문(~해)의 부가의문문: will you?

〔예〕 Study hard, <u>will you</u>? (공부 열심히 해, 그럴 거지?)

4) 청유문(~하자)의 부가의문문: shall we?

〔예〕 Let's go out and play, <u>shall we</u>? (나가서 놀자, 그럴까?)

다음 문장의 부가의문문을 빈칸에 쓰고, 대답을 주어진 조건에 맞추어 쓰시오.
(①번을 참고)

① A: Tom Cruise is handsome, __isn't he__?

B: <u>Yes</u>, <u>he</u> <u>is</u>. (긍정)

② A: She is sad, _____ _____?

B: _____, _____ _____. (부정)

③ A: It is not cheap, _____ it?

B: _____, _____ _____. (긍정)

④ A: He didn't do his homework, _____ _____?

B: _____, _____ _____. (부정)

⑤ A: John doesn't live in Canada, _____ _____?

B: _____, _____ _____. (긍정)

⑥ A: Come home now, _____ _____?

B: _____, _____ _____. (긍정)

A 다음 질문의 빈칸에 부가의문문을 쓰고, 대답으로 빈칸에 Yes/No 중 알맞은 것을 쓰시오.

① A: You are not hungry, _____?

B: _____, I am.

② A: Kevin doesn't work out, _____?

B: _____, he does.

③ A: Jennifer studied hard last weekend, _____?

B: _____, she didn't.

β 다음 우리말에 맞게 빈칸을 적절한 영단어로 채우시오.

① 너는 어제 영어 공부하지 않았지, 그렇지?

You _____ _____ _____ yesterday, _____ _____?

② 너는 거기에 없었어, 그렇지?

You were _____ _____, _____ _____?

③ 내 생일 파티에 와, 그럴 거지?

_____ to my _____ _____, _____ _____?

④ 그녀는 파란색을 좋아하지, 그렇지 않니?

She _____ _____, _____ _____?

A. 다음 빈칸에 ①번처럼 부가의문문을 쓰시오.

① You liked it, <u>didn't you</u> ?

② You were happy, _____?

③ She wasn't sick, _____?

④ Study hard, _____?

⑤ Let's go out and play, _____?

⑥ You are hungry, _____?

⑦ Kevin doesn't work out, _____?

⑧ Jennifer studied hard last weekend, _____?

B. 다음 우리말을 보고 영작하시오.

⑨ 너는 어제 영어 공부하지 않았지, 그렇지?

_____

⑩ 너는 거기에 없었어, 그렇지?

_____

⑪ 내 생일 파티에 와, 그럴 거지?

_____

⑫ 그녀는 파란색을 좋아하지, 그렇지 않니?

_____

정답 ② weren't you ③ was she ④ will you ⑤ shall we ⑥ aren't you ⑦ does he ⑧ didn't she ⑨ You didn't study English yesterday, did you? ⑩ You were not there, were you? ⑪ Come to my birthday party, will you? ⑫ She likes blue, doesn't she?

조동사 can

 혼공개념 | 조동사 can이란?

1 조동사 can : 동사 앞에서 '~할 수 있다, ~해도 된다'라는 의미로 동사를 도와줌

1) 가능: ~할 수 있다(= be able to)

　[예] I can play the piano.

　　　Jimmy can ski.

2) 허락: ~해도 된다

　[예] You can leave now.

　　　You can bring food here.

혼공 팁

조동사 뒤에 오는 동사는 s, es, ed, d가 붙지 않는 '동사원형'을 써야 한다.
[예] Jimmy can ski. (skies, skied X)

3) 부정: cannot 또는 can't

　[예] You cannot use my phone. (cannot = can't)

4) 의문문: can과 주어의 위치를 바꿈

　[예] You can eat this. 　⇒ 　Can you eat this?

　　대답: 긍정 Yes, I can. 　　부정 No, I can't.

5) 부가의문문: 문장 끝에 can 또는 can't를 사용

　[예] You can drive a car, can't you?

　　대답: 긍정 Yes, I can. 　　부정 No, I can't.

A 다음 문장을 not으로 부정하시오.

① He can speak English. _____

② I can move these boxes. _____

③ She can play the flute. _____

④ Mr. Kim can fix the problem. _____

⑤ I can remember their names. _____

β 다음 문장을 의문문으로 만드시오.

① She can speak French. _____

② You can see the stars. _____

③ She can play soccer. _____

④ Paul can swim. _____

⑤ He can teach Korean. _____

⑥ You can eat kimchi. _____

A 다음 문장에 주어진 can이나 can't을 넣어 다시 쓰시오.

① My mom cooks really well.

_____ (can)

② He uses chopsticks.

_____ (can't)

③ You go to bed now.

_____ (can)

B 다음 우리말에 맞게 빈칸을 적절한 영단어로 채우시오.

① 당신은 나와 춤을 출 수 있나요?

_____ _____ _____ with me?

② 당신은 나를 위해 노래를 한 곡 부를 수 있나요?

_____ _____ _____ a song for me?

③ 저는 노래 부를 수도 있고 춤을 출 수도 있어요.

I _____ _____ and _____.

④ 우리는 저 영화 볼 수 없지, 그렇지?

_____ _____ _____ the movie, _____ _____?

A. 다음 문장을 부정하시오.

① He can speak English. _____

② I can move these boxes. _____

③ She can play the flute. _____

B. 다음 문장을 의문문으로 만드시오.

④ He can speak French. _____

⑤ You can see the stars. _____

⑥ She can play soccer. _____

C. 다음 우리말을 보고 영작하시오.

⑦ 저는 노래 부를 수도 있고 춤을 출 수도 있어요.

_____

⑧ 우리는 저 영화 볼 수 없지, 그렇지?

_____

⑨ 그는 젓가락을 사용할 수 없다.

_____

⑩ 너는 지금 잠자리에 들 수 없다.

_____

정답 ① He can't(cannot) speak English. ② I can't(cannot) move these boxes. ③ She can't(cannot) play the flute. ④ Can he speak French? ⑤ Can you see the stars? ⑥ Can she play soccer? ⑦ I can sing and dance. ⑧ We can't(cannot) watch the movie, can we? ⑨ He can't(cannot) use chopsticks. ⑩ You can't(cannot) go to bed now.

조동사 will

 혼공개념 조동사 will이란?

1 조동사 will : 동사 앞에서 '~할 것이다'라는 의미로 쓰이며, 말하는 사람의 '의지나 앞으로의 일'에 대해 표현함

[예] I will go see a doctor in the afternoon.

I will be a scientist.

1) 부정: will not(won't)

[예] I will not(won't) make these mistakes again.

2) 여러 가지 축약형(줄임형)

[예] I will = I'll　　You will = You'll　　He will = He'll

She will = She'll　　They will = They'll　　It will = It'll

3) 의문문 만들기: will과 주어의 위치를 바꿈

[예] You will bring your lunch. ⇒ Will you bring your lunch?

대답: 긍정 Yes, I will.　　　　부정 No, I won't.

혼공 팁

will과 be going to은 '~할 것이다'라는 같은 뜻을 가지고 있다. 하지만 will은 '다짐', '의지'가 강조된 표현이고 be going to는 '구체적인 계획'이 있을 때 많이 쓴다.

[예] I will visit Spain.(단순 의지)

I am going to visit Spain.(구체적 계획)

A 다음 문장을 not으로 부정하시오.

① I will go see a doctor. _____

② I will be a scientist. _____

③ They will come soon. _____

④ I will go to the party. _____

⑤ He will bring his lunch. _____

B 다음 문장을 의문문으로 만드시오.

① You will bring your lunch. _____

② You will clean the house. _____

③ He will eat vegetables. _____

④ He will drive my car. _____

⑤ You will visit her place. _____

⑥ John will love this gift. _____

A 다음 우리말에 맞게 빈칸을 적절한 영단어로 채우시오.

① 내가 그에게 책을 읽어 줄게.

I _____ _____ him a book.

② 우리는 금요일에 외식할 것이다.

We _____ _____ out this Friday.

③ Kevin은 문을 닫을 것이다.

Kevin _____ _____ the door.

B 다음 A의 말에 이어질 B의 대답을 완성하시오.

① A: You are late again!

B: I'm so sorry. I _____ _____ late again.

② A: What will you do after school?

B: I _____ _____ _____. (badminton)

③ A: It's time to go to bed, Dan.

B: Okay. I _____ _____ _____ _____ soon.

④ A: What will the weather be like tomorrow?

B: It _____ _____ _____ tomorrow. (sunny)

A. 다음 문장을 부정하시오.

① I will go see a doctor. _____

② I will be a scientist. _____

③ They will come soon. _____

B. 다음 문장을 의문문으로 만드시오.

④ You will bring your lunch. _____

⑤ You will clean the house. _____

⑥ You will visit her place. _____

C. 다음 우리말을 보고 영작하시오.

⑦ 우리는 금요일에 외식할 것이다.

_____

⑧ 나는 배드민턴을 칠 것이다.

_____

정답 ① I will not(won't) go see a doctor. ② I will not(won't) be a scientist. ③ They will not(won't) come soon. ④ Will you bring your lunch? ⑤ Will you clean the house? ⑥ Will you visit her place? ⑦ We will eat out this Friday. ⑧ I will play badminton.

조동사 may

1 조동사 may : 동사 앞에서 '~해도 된다, ~일지도 모른다'라는 의미로 쓰이는 조동사

 1) 허락 : ~해도 된다

  예 You may ask my age.

    May I help you?

 2) 약한 추측: ~일지도 모른다

  예 He may be sick.   She may be right.

    It may be true.

 3) 부정문 만들기: may not(주로 may가 추측의 의미일 때 많이 쓰임)

  예 He <u>may not</u> be sick.

    She <u>may not</u> be right.

 4) 의문문 만들기: may와 주어의 위치를 바꿈

  예 <u>I</u> <u>may</u> ask you a question.   ⇒   <u>May</u> <u>I</u> ask you a question?

   대답: 긍정 Yes, you may.   부정 No, you may not.

  혼공 팁

  may not은 축약형이 따로 없다. mayn't (X)

A 다음 문장에서 쓰인 may의 뜻이 '약한 추측'인지 '허락'인지 선택하시오.

① He may be rich. (약한 추측 / 허락)

② You may go home. (약한 추측 / 허락)

③ It may snow tomorrow. (약한 추측 / 허락)

④ May I use your phone? (약한 추측 / 허락)

β 다음 문장을 not을 써서 부정문으로 만드시오.

① He may be rich. _____

② It may be true. _____

③ It may snow tomorrow. _____

④ They may be very poor. _____

C 다음 문장을 의문문으로 만드시오.

① I may use the computer. _____

② I may go home. _____

A 다음 우리말과 일치하도록 괄호 안의 단어를 사용하여 빈칸을 채우시오.

① 그는 감기에 걸릴지도 몰라.

He _____ _____ a cold. (catch)

② 오늘 비가 올지도 몰라.

It _____ _____ today. (rain)

③ 그녀는 아픈지도 몰라.

She _____ _____ _____. (be)

β 다음 주어진 말들을 의미에 맞게 배열하고, 주어진 조건에 맞추어 대답하시오.

① (I / turn on / may / the TV) ?

_____?

긍정의 대답: Yes, _____.

② (wait / I / in the office / may) ?

_____?

부정의 대답: No, _____.

③ (sit down / may / I / here) ?

_____?

긍정의 대답: Yes, _____.

A. 다음 문장을 부정하시오.

① He may be rich. _____

② You may go home. _____

③ It may snow tomorrow. _____

B. 다음 문장을 의문문으로 만드시오.

④ I may use the computer. _____

⑤ I may go home. _____

C. 다음 우리말을 보고 영작하시오.

⑥ 그는 감기에 걸릴지도 몰라.

_____

⑦ 오늘 비가 올지도 몰라.

_____

⑧ 그녀는 아픈지도 몰라.

_____

정답 ① He may not be rich. ② You may not go home. ③ It may not snow tomorrow. ④ May I use the computer? ⑤ May I go home? ⑥ He may catch a cold. ⑦ It may rain today. ⑧ She may be sick.

조동사 must

혼공개념 조동사 must란?

1 조동사 must : 동사 앞에서 '반드시 ~해야 한다, ~인 게 틀림없다'라는 의미로 쓰이는 조동사

1) 강한 의무: 반드시 ~해야 한다

[예] You must buy a ticket.

You must not park here.

2) 강한 추측: ~인 게 틀림없다

[예] It must be true.   It must not be true.

She must be happy.

혼공 팁

must와 비슷한 의미를 가진 표현에 have to가 있다. must는 굉장히 강하게 들리기 때문에
적절한 '강제, 의무'를 나타낼 때 have to를 많이 쓴다.

[예] You have to go there by 6.

You <u>don't</u> have to go there by 6.(부정)

3) 의문문 만들기

[예] I must take vitamins every day.

⇒ Must I take vitamins every day?

대답: 긍정 Yes, you must.   부정 No, you must not.

I have to take vitamins every day.

⇒ Do I have to take vitamins every day?

A 다음 문장을 not 또는 don't으로 부정하시오.

① You must buy a ticket.

_____

② You must park here.

_____

③ You have to go there by 6.

_____

β 다음 문장을 의문문으로 만드시오.

① I have to take vitamins every day.

_____

② I have to water the garden today.

_____

C 다음 문장에서 쓰인 must의 뜻이 '강한 추측' 인지 '강한 의무' 인지 선택하시오.

① He must leave now.　　　　(강한 추측 / 강한 의무)

② He must be happy.　　　　(강한 추측 / 강한 의무)

③ It must be true.　　　　(강한 추측 / 강한 의무)

다음 우리말과 일치하도록 빈칸을 채우시오.

① 너는 콜라를 마셔서는 안 돼.

You _____ _____ _____ coke.

② 나는 지금 반드시 학교에 가야 해.

I _____ _____ to school now.

③ John은 지금 그녀에게 반드시 전화해야 한다.

John _____ _____ her now.

β 다음 표지판을 보고 빈칸에 알맞은 말을 쓰시오.

①   You _____ _____ here.

②    You _____ _____ _____ here.

③    You _____ _____ _____ your pet. (bring)

 다음 John의 말에 알맞은 나의 대답을 완성하시오.

John: Hey, must I wear this helmet?

나 : _____, _____ _____. It's dangerous here.

A. 다음 문장을 부정하시오.

① You must buy a ticket.

_____

② You must park here.

_____

③ You have to go there by 6.

_____

B. 다음 우리말을 보고 영작하시오.

④ 너는 콜라를 마셔서는 안 돼.

_____

⑤ 나는 지금 반드시 학교에 가야 해.

_____

⑥ John은 지금 그녀에게 반드시 전화해야 한다.

_____

정답 ① You must not buy a ticket. ② You must not park here. ③ You don't have to go there by 6. ④ You must not drink coke. ⑤ I must go to school now. ⑥ John must call her now.

형용사의 용법

혼공개념 형용사란?

1 형용사: 사물이나 사람의 모습, 상태를 설명해 주는 단어

예 nice, cold, hot, good, great, tall, expensive...

a <u>nice</u> <u>car</u>　　　멋진(형용사) 자동차

1) 명사 앞에서 꾸며주는 형용사(한정적 용법): ~한, ~ㄴ

예 Steve is a <u>cool</u> <u>guy</u>.

The <u>pretty</u> <u>girl</u> is my sister.

2) 'be동사+형용사'로 풀어서 말하는 형용사(서술적 용법): ~이다, ~다(덩어리로 해석)

예 Steve <u>is cool</u>.

The novel <u>is interesting</u>.

It <u>is expensive</u>.

혼공 연습

A 다음 우리말과 일치하도록 빈칸을 채우시오.

① 값싼 자전거   a _____ bicycle

② 예쁜 소녀   a _____ _____

③ 키 큰 남자   a _____ guy

B 다음 우리말과 일치하도록 빈칸을 채우시오.

① 그것은 비싸다.   It _____ _____.

② 그것은 매웠다.   It _____ _____.

③ 그것들은 길었다. They _____ _____.

C 다음 우리말과 일치하도록 빈칸을 채우시오.

① 그것은 값싼 자전거이다.   It is a _____ _____.

② 그 예쁜 소녀는 내 여동생이다.   The _____ _____ is ____ sister.

③ 그 소설은 흥미로웠다.   The novel ____ _____.

④ 그의 농담들은 재미있었다.   His jokes _____ _____.

A 다음 우리말과 일치하도록 빈칸을 채우시오.

① 나의 선생님들은 똑똑하시다.

My _____ _____ _____. (smart)

② 그것은 빨간색(의) 자동차이다.

It is a _____ _____.

③ 그 집은 크다.

The house _____ _____.

④ 그들은 정직했다.

_____ _____ _____.

B 주어진 단어를 <보기>처럼 의미에 맞게 배열하시오.

<보기>   nurse / is / a / kind / Suzy   →   Suzy is a kind nurse.

① Tom / a / student / good / is   _____

② are / they / clever   _____

③ is / interesting / French   _____

④ this show / boring / is   _____

⑤ healthy / is / Alex   _____

A. 다음 우리말을 영어로 옮기시오.

① 값싼 자전거   a _____ bicycle

② 예쁜 소녀   a _____ _____

③ 키 큰 남자   a _____ guy

④ 그것은 비싸다.   It _____ _____.

⑤ 그것은 매웠다.   It _____ _____.

⑥ 그것들은 길었다.   They _____ _____.

B. 다음 우리말을 보고 영작하시오.

⑦ 나의 선생님들은 똑똑하시다.

     My _____ _____ _____.

⑧ 그것은 빨간색(의) 자동차이다.

     It is a _____ _____.

⑨ 그 집은 크다.

     The house _____ _____.

⑩ 그들은 정직했다.

     _____ _____ _____.

정답 ① cheap ② pretty, girl ③ tall ④ is, expensive ⑤ was, hot(spicy) ⑥ were, long ⑦ teachers, are, smart ⑧ red, car ⑨ is, big
⑩ They, were, honest

수량 형용사 1

1 많음을 의미하는 수량 형용사: many, much, a lot of(=lots of)

1) many : '많은'을 의미하고 셀 수 있는 명사를 수식

　예 I bought <u>many</u> <u>books</u>.

　　　I can see <u>many</u> <u>stars</u> at night.

2) much : '많은'을 의미하고 셀 수 없는 명사를 수식

　예 She put <u>much</u> <u>sugar</u> in the soup.

　　　The rich man keeps <u>much</u> <u>money</u> in his safe.

3) a lot of(=lots of) : '많은'을 의미하고 셀 수 있는 명사, 셀 수 없는 명사를 모두 수식
　　　　　　　　　　할 수 있음

　예 There were <u>a lot of</u> animals in the zoo.

　　　I have <u>a lot of</u> <u>work</u> today.

4) How many ~? / How much ~? : '얼마나 많은 ~?'의 뜻으로 many 다음에는 셀 수 있
　　　　　　　　　　　　　　　는 명사, much 다음에는 셀 수 없는 명사가 옴

　예 <u>How many</u> <u>people</u> are there?

　　　<u>How much</u> <u>money</u> do you have?

A 다음 우리말과 일치하도록 <보기>를 참고하여 빈칸을 채우시오.

<보기>　　　　많은 자동차들　⇒　<u>many cars (a lot of cars)</u>

① 많은 사과들　　　_____

② 많은 돈　　　　　_____

③ 많은 일　　　　　_____

④ 많은 동물들　　　_____

⑤ 많은 설탕　　　　_____

ß 다음 우리말과 일치하도록 빈칸을 채우시오.

① 그녀는 많은 설탕을 찌개에 넣었다.

　　She put _____ _____ in the soup.

② 그 부자는 많은 돈을 그의 금고에 가지고 있다.

　　The rich man keeps _____ _____ in his _____.

③ 나는 오늘 일이 많다.

　　I have _____ _____ _____ _____ today.

④ 동물원에 동물들이 많이 있었다.

　　There _____ _____ _____ _____ animals in the _____.

A 다음 <보기>처럼 완성된 문장을 만드시오.

> <보기>　islands in the Philippines
> 　　⇒ There are a lot of islands in the Philippines.

① kangaroos in Australia

　_____

② people in Seoul

　_____

③ items in the supermarket

　_____

B How many와 How much를 사용해서 <보기>처럼 의문문을 만드시오.

> <보기>　friends do you have
> 　　⇒ How many friends do you have?

① money do you have 　　　_____

② time do you have 　　　_____

③ brothers and sisters do you have

　_____

A. 다음 우리말을 ①처럼 영어로 옮기시오.

① 많은 사과들   many (a lot of=lots of) apples

② 많은 돈   _____

③ 많은 일   _____

④ 많은 동물들   _____

⑤ 많은 설탕   _____

B. 다음 우리말을 보고 영작하시오.

⑥ 그녀는 많은 설탕을 찌개에 넣었다.

_____

⑦ 그 부자는 많은 돈을 그의 금고에 가지고 있다.

_____

⑧ 나는 오늘 일이 많다.

_____

⑨ 동물원에 동물들이 많이 있었다.

_____

정답 ② much(a lot of=lots of) money ③ much(a lot of=lots of) work ④ many(a lot of=lots of) animals ⑤ much(a lot of=lots of) sugar ⑥ She put much(a lot of=lots of) sugar in the soup. ⑦ The rich man keeps much(a lot of=lots of) money in his safe. ⑧ I have much(a lot of=lots of) work today. ⑨ There were many(a lot of=lots of) animals in the zoo.

수량 형용사 2

혼공개념   수량 형용사 few, a few, little, a little이란?

	셀 수 있는 명사	셀 수 없는 명사
조금 있는(긍정)	a few	a little
거의 없는(부정)	few	little

예 I need <u>a few things</u>.

There is <u>a little bread</u>.

There are <u>few people</u> on the stage.

There is <u>little water</u> in the bottle.

혼공개념   some, any란?

	some	any
의미	약간의, 조금의	
쓰이는 곳	긍정문, 확인, 부탁이나 권유를 하는 의문문	부정문, 조건문, 대부분의 의문문, 부정의 단어가 있는 경우
	셀 수 있는 명사, 셀 수 없는 명사 모두 수식 가능	

예 There is <u>some water</u>.   I got <u>some letters</u> from them.

Will you have <u>some coffee</u>?   Do you have <u>any money</u>?

There aren't <u>any buses</u> on Sunday.   She refused <u>any help</u>.

If you have <u>any questions</u>, please ask me.

A 빈칸에 a few 혹은 a little을 쓰시오.

① _____ bananas   _____ cheese

② _____ grapes   _____ coffee

③ _____ water   _____ monkeys

④ _____ books   _____ sandwiches

β 다음 우리말과 일치하도록 빈칸을 few, a few, little, a little 중 적절한 것으로 채우시오.

① 나는 몇 개의 물건들이 필요하다.

I need _____ _____ things.

② 나는 돈이 조금 있다.

I have _____ _____ money.

③ 무대에는 사람들이 거의 없다.

There are _____ _____ on the stage.

④ 병에 물이 거의 없다.

There is _____ _____ in the bottle.

A <보기>처럼 문장을 만드시오.

> <보기>　　meat　⇒　There is some meat.

① milk _____

② spoons _____

③ eggs _____

B 빈칸에 few, a few, little, a little 중 적절한 것을 골라 쓰시오.

① I have _____ money, so I can buy this.

② There is _____ water in the pool. We can't swim.

③ She is lonely. She has _____ friends.

④ His writing is perfect. It has _____ mistakes.

C 빈칸에 some, any 중 하나를 골라 쓰시오.

① Can I get you _____ wine?

② I can't find _____ children now.

③ If you make _____ mistakes, please tell me.

④ I have _____ interesting ideas.

⑤ There's _____ mud on the carpet.

⑥ Can you lend me _____ money?

A. few, a few, little, a little 중에 알맞은 표현을 쓰시오.

① 나는 몇 개의 물건들이 필요하다.

I need _____ things.

② 나는 돈이 조금 있다.

I have _____ money.

③ 무대에는 사람들이 거의 없다.

There are _____ people on the stage.

④ 병에 물이 거의 없다.

There is _____ water in the bottle.

B. some, any 중에 알맞은 표현을 쓰시오.

⑤ Can I get you _____ wine?

⑥ I can't find _____ children now.

⑦ If you make _____ mistakes, please tell me.

⑧ I have _____ interesting ideas.

⑨ There's _____ mud on the carpet.

⑩ Can you lend me _____ money?

정답 ① a few ② a little ③ few ④ little ⑤ some ⑥ any ⑦ any ⑧ some ⑨ some ⑩ some

부사 / 빈도부사

부사란?

1 부사: 문장에서 동사, 형용사, 다른 부사, 문장 전체를 꾸미는 말

예 He studies Spanish <u>hard</u>.　　　English is <u>very</u> easy.

　　Thank you <u>very</u> much.　　　　<u>Luckily</u>, she won the lottery.

1) 부사의 형태

원래 부사인 단어	well, now, here, there
형용사 + ly인 단어	slow + ly, careful + ly, kind + ly, beautiful + ly easy + ly = easily (자음 + y)
형용사와 같은 형태를 가진 부사	hard, fast, early, late

빈도부사란?

1 빈도부사: 얼마나 자주 뭔가를 하는지 횟수를 알려주는 부사

never	sometimes	often	usually	always
결코 ~않다	때때로	종종	보통, 대개	항상

예 My students <u>never</u> tell me a lie.

　　I <u>usually</u> take a walk in the morning.

혼공 팁

빈도부사의 위치는 일반적으로 조동사, be동사 뒤, 일반동사 앞이지만 꼭 그렇지는 않다.

혼공 연습

A 다음 단어의 부사 형태를 쓰시오. (형태가 같으면 그대로 쓰시오.)

① slow _____   hard _____

② well _____   now _____

③ kind _____   beautiful _____

④ easy _____   early _____

⑤ fast _____   happy _____

⑥ careful _____   late _____

B 다음 우리말과 일치하도록 빈칸을 채우시오.

① 영어는 아주 쉽다.   English is _____ easy.

② 나는 일찍 잔다.   I go to bed _____.

③ 나의 아버지께서는 조심스럽게 운전하신다.

My father drives _____.

④ 내 학생들은 결코 나에게 거짓말을 하지 않는다.

My students _____ tell me a lie.

⑤ 내 동생은 책을 빨리 읽는다.

My younger brother reads a book _____.

A 다음 주어진 말들을 의미에 맞게 배열하시오.

① he / well / Chinese / speaks _____

② up / get / I / late _____

③ walks / Jason / slowly _____

④ closely / the book / at / look _____

B 다음 우리말과 일치하도록 빈칸을 영어로 채우시오.

① 나는 피아노를 잘 칠 수 있다.　　I _____.

② Tom은 빨리 달릴 수 있다.　　Tom _____.

③ 너는 매일 운동해야 한다.　　You have to _____.

C never, sometimes, often, usually, always 중 한 단어를 알맞은 곳에 넣어 다시 쓰시오.

① My mom gets up late in the morning. (종종)

_____

② I use a red pen. (절대 ~ 않다)

_____

③ He is late for school. (보통)

_____

④ I will love you. (항상)

_____

A. 빈칸에 알맞은 표현을 쓰시오.

① 영어는 아주 쉽다.   English is _____ easy.

② 나는 일찍 잔다.   I go to bed _____.

③ 나의 아버지께서는 조심스럽게 운전하신다.

My father drives _____.

④ 내 학생들은 결코 나에게 거짓말을 하지 않는다.

My students _____ tell me a lie.

⑤ 내 동생은 책을 빨리 읽는다.

My younger brother reads a book _____.

B. 다음 우리말을 보고 영작하시오.

⑥ 나는 피아노를 잘 칠 수 있다.

_____

⑦ 너는 매일 운동해야 한다.

_____

⑧ 나는 절대 빨간색 펜을 쓰지 않는다.

_____

⑨ 그는 학교에 보통 지각한다.

_____

정답 ① very ② early ③ carefully ④ never ⑤ fast ⑥ I can play the piano well. ⑦ You have to exercise(work out) every day.
⑧ I never use a red pen. ⑨ He is usually late for school.

what / how 감탄문

 혼공개념 감탄문이란?

1 감탄문: 기쁘고, 놀라고, 슬플 때 강한 감정을 표현하는 문장

   1) What 감탄문: What + (a / an) + 형용사 + 명사 + (주어 + 동사)!

     [예] What a nice day it is!

       = It is a very nice day.

       What exciting games they are!

        = They are very exciting games.

   2) How 감탄문: How + 형용사/부사 + (주어 + 동사)!

     [예] How handsome Mr. Kim is!

       = Mr. Kim is very handsome.

       How fast the horse runs!

       = The horse runs very fast.

혼공 팁

what 감탄문은 주로 명사 덩어리와 결합하고, how 감탄문은 부사나 형용사와 결합한다는 것이 결정적 차이이다.

What <u>a nice day</u> it is!   How <u>fast</u> the horse runs!

   날씨 좋은 날   빨리

혼공 연습

A 단어를 알맞게 배열하여 감탄문을 만드시오.

① is / a / nice / it / what / day _____ !

② what / games / they / exciting / are

_____ !

③ handsome / how / is / Mr. Kim

_____ !

④ the horse / fast / how / runs

_____ !

B 다음 <보기>처럼 how 감탄문을 만드시오.

<보기>　　tall, he ⇒ How tall he is!

① smart, she _____

② delicious, it _____

③ diligent, he _____

C 다음 <보기>처럼 what 감탄문을 만드시오.

<보기>　　an exciting game ⇒ What an exciting game it is!

① a cute cat _____

② a kind boy _____

③ tall buildings _____

A 다음 괄호 안에서 알맞은 것을 고르시오.

① (How / What) a pretty girl Chloe is!

② (How / What) beautifully she dances!

③ (How / What) fast he runs!

④ (How / What) special gifts they are!

⑤ (How / What) beautiful the garden is!

⑥ (How / What) interesting the show is!

B 다음 빈칸에 알맞은 단어를 쓰시오.

① A: I will give you a ride to school.

B: _____ kind you are!

② A: I paid $1,000 for these comic books.

B: _____ _____ they are!

C 다음을 알맞게 배열하여 감탄문을 만드시오.

① difficult / how / the question / is

_____!

② noisy / the kids / how / are

_____!

A. 빈칸에 What, How 중 알맞은 단어를 쓰시오.

① _____ a nice day it is!

② _____ exciting games they are!

③ _____ handsome Mr. Kim is!

④ _____ tall he is!

B. 다음 단어를 참고하여 how 감탄문을 만드시오.

⑤ smart, she → _____!

⑥ delicious, it → _____!

⑦ diligent, he → _____!

C. How, What 중 알맞은 단어를 선택하시오.

⑧ (How / What) a pretty girl Chloe is!

⑨ (How / What) beautifully she dances!

⑩ (How / What) fast he runs!

⑪ (How / What) special gifts they are!

⑫ (How / What) beautiful the house is!

⑬ (How / What) interesting the show is!

정답 ① What ② What ③ How ④ How ⑤ How smart she is ⑥ How delicious it is ⑦ How diligent he is ⑧ What ⑨ How ⑩ How ⑪ What ⑫ How ⑬ How

비인칭 주어 it

 혼공개념 | 비인칭 주어란?

1 비인칭 주어 it: 뜻이 없는 주어의 역할을 하는 it

1) 날씨

   예 <u>It</u> is really hot today.

2) 시각

   예 <u>It</u> is 7 o'clock.

3) 요일

   예 <u>It</u> is Monday.

4) 날짜

   예 <u>It</u> is December 24.

5) 거리

   예 <u>It</u> is 10km from here to my place.

6) 명암

   예 <u>It</u> is dark outside.

혼 공 팁

대명사 it은 말하는 사물, 사실이 분명하지만, 비인칭 주어는 위의 용법으로만 쓰인다.

예 A: Where is my book?   A: He passed the test.

   B: <u>It</u> is on the table.(대명사)   B: <u>It</u> is true.(대명사)

A 다음 문장에서 쓰인 비인칭 주어 it의 알맞은 쓰임을 <보기>에서 찾아 쓰시오.

> <보기>   날씨, 시각, 요일, 날짜, 명암, 거리

① It is December 24.   _____

② It is Monday.   _____

③ It is 7 o'clock.   _____

④ It is really hot today.   _____

⑤ It is dark outside.   _____

⑥ It is 10km from here to my place.   _____

β 다음 밑줄 친 it이 대명사인지 비인칭 주어인지 <보기>처럼 빈칸에 쓰시오.

> <보기>   A: Where is my book?
> B: It is on the table.   대명사

① A: What is the date today?

　 B: It is March 15.   _____

② A: He passed the test.

　 B: It is true.   _____

③ A: How is the weather?

　 B: It is sunny.   _____

다음 사진을 보고 알맞은 표현을 영어로 쓰시오.

① _____ is very _____ today.

② _____ is _____.

③ _____ is _____.

 다음 우리말을 영어로 옮기시오.

① 4월이다.   It _____.

② 토요일이다.   It _____.

③ (날씨가) 화창하다.   It _____.

④ 내 아파트에서 2킬로미터이다.   _____ from my apartment.

A. 다음 문장에서 쓰인 비인칭 주어 it의 알맞은 쓰임을 아래 <보기>에서 찾아 쓰시오.

<보기>	날씨, 시각, 요일, 날짜, 명암, 거리

① It is December 24. ＿＿＿＿＿＿

② It is Monday. ＿＿＿＿＿＿

③ It is 7 o'clock. ＿＿＿＿＿＿

④ It is really hot today. ＿＿＿＿＿＿

⑤ It is dark outside. ＿＿＿＿＿＿

⑥ It is 10km from here to my place. ＿＿＿＿＿＿

B. 다음 우리말을 영어로 옮기시오.

⑦ 4월이다. It ＿＿＿＿＿＿＿＿＿.

⑧ 토요일이다. It ＿＿＿＿＿＿＿＿＿.

⑨ (날씨가) 화창하다. It ＿＿＿＿＿＿＿＿＿.

⑩ 내 아파트에서 2킬로미터이다. ＿＿＿＿＿＿＿ from my apartment.

정답 ① 날짜 ② 요일 ③ 시각 ④ 날씨 ⑤ 명암 ⑥ 거리 ⑦ is April ⑧ is Saturday ⑨ is sunny ⑩ It is 2km(kilometers)

시간을 나타내는 전치사

1 시간을 나타내는 전치사: 주로 시간을 나타내는 명사 앞에서 '~에'라는 의미로 쓰임

　1) at을 쓰는 경우: 주로 특정 시간, 시각 앞

　　예 at 6, at night, at noon

　　　I sometimes take a walk <u>at night</u>.

　2) in을 쓰는 경우: 달, 계절, 연도, 세기(Century) 앞

　　예 He is going to come back to Korea <u>in April</u>.

　　　It rains a lot <u>in summer</u>.

　　　I was born <u>in 2002</u>.

　　　World war II ended <u>in the 20th century</u>.

혼공 팁

in은 비교적 큰 단위 앞에 쓰지만, 그렇지 않은 경우도 있다.
예 in the morning, in the evening
in + 시간(~후에 : in 10 minutes)
I'll be back <u>in an hour</u>.

　3) on을 쓰는 경우: 요일, 특정한 날

　　예 I play tennis <u>on Mondays</u>.

　　　She goes hiking <u>on weekends</u>.

　　　She went to America <u>on June 14</u>.

혼공 연습

A 다음 빈칸에 at, in, on 중 하나를 쓰시오.

① _____ 7 o'clock   _____ night

② _____ September   _____ noon

③ _____ summer   _____ Mondays

④ _____ 2004   _____ weekends

⑤ _____ May 1   _____ the morning

⑥ _____ 10 minutes   _____ 4 weeks

⑦ _____ two hours   _____ 2 minutes

⑧ _____ winter   _____ February 3

⑨ _____ the afternoon   _____ half an hour

B 다음 빈칸에 at, in, on 중 하나를 쓰시오.

① I usually get up _____ 7 o'clock.

② My birthday is _____ December.

③ He goes hiking _____ Saturdays.

④ It is hot _____ summer.

⑤ Our vacation starts _____ July.

⑥ He will come back _____ 5 minutes.

A 다음 우리말을 참고하여 빈칸을 채우시오.

① Jun은 일요일마다 영어를 공부한다.

Jun _____ English _____ _____.

② 내 부모님들께서는 9시에 집을 나가신다.

My parents leave _____ ____ 9:00.

③ 그녀는 겨울에 스노보드 타는 것을 즐긴다.

She _____ snowboarding _____ _____.

④ 그는 30분 뒤에 학교에 갈 것이다.

He will _____ to _____ _____ 30 minutes.

β 주어진 표현을 의미에 맞게 배열하시오.

① the morning / to the movies / I / in / went

_____

② night / books / reads / at / he

_____

③ was born / 1970 / my / in / father

_____

④ doesn't / night / she / anything / eat / at

_____

A. 다음 빈칸에 at, in, on 중에 하나를 쓰시오.

① _____ 7 o'clock   _____ night   _____ September

② _____ noon   _____ summer   _____ Mondays

③ _____ May 1   _____ the morning   _____ 4 weeks

④ _____ two hours   _____ 2004   _____ weekends

⑤ I usually get up _____ 7 o'clock.

⑥ My birthday is _____ December.

⑦ He goes hiking _____ Saturdays.

⑧ It is hot _____ summer.

⑨ Our vacation starts _____ July.

⑩ He will come back _____ 5 minutes.

B. 주어진 표현을 의미에 맞게 배열하시오.

⑪ night / books / reads / at / he

_____

⑫ was born / 1970 / my / in / father

_____

⑬ doesn't / night / she / anything / eat / at

_____

정답 ① at, at, in ② at, in, on ③ on, in, in ④ in, in, on ⑤ at ⑥ in ⑦ on ⑧ in ⑨ in ⑩ in ⑪ He reads books at night. ⑫ My father was born in 1970. ⑬ She doesn't eat anything at night.

장소를 나타내는 전치사

1 장소를 나타내는 전치사: 명사 앞에서 다양한 의미로 쓰여 장소나 위치를 나타냄

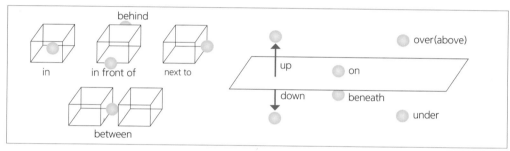

[예] Tom is <u>in his room</u>.

A cat is <u>on the sofa</u>.

There is a bridge <u>above(over)</u> the river.

Kevin sits <u>next to</u> me.

He disappeared <u>in front of</u> my eyes.

There is a yard <u>behind</u> the house.

I found the key <u>under</u> the table.

혼공 팁

at과 in은 둘 다 '~에'라는 뜻으로 혼동하기 쉽다. at은 '어떤 지점'을 말할 때, in은 보통 '공간, 지역, 말하는 사람과 밀접한 연관'을 나타낼 때 주로 쓴다.

[예] Let's meet in Seoul.

I was born in Seoul.

You have to study hard at school.

She is watching TV in the living room.

A 다음 우리말을 참고하여 빈칸에 들어갈 전치사 또는 표현을 쓰시오.

① Tom은 그의 방안에 있다.   Tom is _____ his room.

② 고양이가 소파 위에 있다.   A cat is _____ the sofa.

③ 강 위에 다리가 하나 있다.

There is a bridge _____ the river.

④ Kevin은 내 옆에 앉는다.

Kevin sits _____ me.

⑤ 그는 내 눈 앞에서 사라졌다.

He disappeared _____ my eyes.

⑥ 집 뒤에는 마당이 있다.

There is a yard _____ the house.

⑦ 나는 그 탁자 아래에서 열쇠 하나를 발견했다.

I found a key _____ the table.

B 다음 빈칸에 알맞은 전치사 또는 표현을 쓰시오.

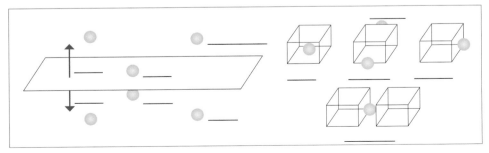

A 다음 질문에 대한 답을 영어로 쓰시오.

① Where is your mom? _____ (거실에)

② Where is your wallet? _____ (책상 위에)

③ Where is my cell phone? _____ (내 가방 안에)

④ Where is Melanie? _____ (커튼 뒤에)

B 다음 <보기>처럼 전치사 표현을 덧붙여서 문장을 완성하시오.

<보기> a fly / is / the wall / there → There is a fly on the wall.

① a gas stove / is / there / the kitchen

_____

② are / his office / there / a lot of / computers

_____

③ were / they / Gwangju / born

_____

④ met / him / I / the airport

_____

⑤ he / the park / is taking a walk

_____

A. 다음 빈칸에 알맞은 전치사 또는 표현을 쓰시오.

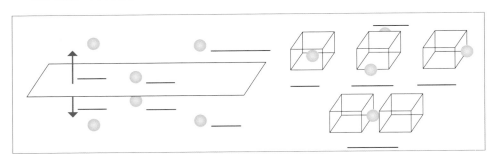

B. 빈칸에 들어갈 전치사 또는 표현을 쓰시오.

① Kevin은 내 옆에 앉는다.　　　　　Kevin sits _____ _____ me.

② 집 뒤에는 마당이 있다.　　　　　There is a yard _____ the house.

③ 나는 그 탁자 아래에서 열쇠 하나를 발견했다.

　　　I found a key _____ the table.

C. 주어진 단어를 의미에 맞게 배열하시오.

④ in / a gas stove / is / there / the kitchen

_____

⑤ in his office / are / there / a lot of / computers

_____

⑥ were / in / they / Gwangju / born

_____

⑦ at / met / him / I / the airport

_____

혼공 기초 영문법
LEVEL 1
정답

명사의 수

Part 1

A ①water ②bread ③luggage ④money ⑤Chloe

B ①Jun ②water ③love ④furniture ⑤cheese ⑥Kevin ⑦furniture

Part 2

A 셀 수 있는 명사: apple, banana, child, computer
셀 수 없는 명사: milk, water, money, beauty, ham, cheese, sugar, salt, paper, love, pride, courage, happiness, furniture

B ①two, eggs ②luck ③water, milk ④loaf, bread, two, slices, cheese

 명사의 복수형태 만들기

Part 1

A ①boats, hats, carrots ②buses, classes, axes ③churches, dishes, potatoes ④days, boys, toys ⑤monkeys, flies, cities ⑥babies, leaves, knives ⑦men, children, teeth ⑧feet, women

B ①glasses ②scissors ③pants ④chopsticks ⑤pajamas

Part 2

A families, benches, women

B ①apples ②monkeys ③five leaves

C ①pianos ②potatoes ③pajamas ④days

 인칭대명사의 주격/소유격

Part 1

A ①I, my ②you, your ③he, his ④she, her ⑤it, its ⑥we, our ⑦you, your ⑧they, their

B ①my ②your ③you ④he, her ⑤she, his ⑥it, Joe's ⑦we, its ⑧Jason, their

Part 2

A ①It ②I ③She ④her ⑤I, her ⑥They, his ⑦He, his ⑧They, its

B ①her ②Kevin's ③Kevin, his ④I, their

 인칭대명사의 목적격

Part 1

A ①I, me ②you, you ③his, him ④her, her ⑤it, it ⑥we, us ⑦your, you ⑧their, them

B ①him ②it ③us ④he, them ⑤she, it ⑥it, Joe ⑦Kevin, you ⑧they, Jason

Part 2

A ①them ②me ③us ④her ⑤I, Mr. Kim ⑥She, you ⑦He, his, it ⑧Her, them

B ①her ②it ③them ④She, us

 소유대명사

Part 1

A ①my, mine ②you, yours ③his, his ④her, hers ⑤its, it ⑥us, ours ⑦you, yours ⑧them, theirs

B ①mine ②hers ③yours ④his ⑤ours ⑥theirs ⑦mine, hers

Part 2

A ①mine ②yours ③theirs ④his ⑤He, ours ⑥It, theirs ⑦hers

B ①theirs ②hers ③ours ④mine

 be동사의 현재형

Part 1

A ①am, are, is ②is, is, are ③are, are, is ④am, is, are ⑤are, are, is ⑥is, are, am

B 본문 31쪽 표를 참고하세요.

Part 2

A ①am ②is ③are

B ①Julian is not young. ②They are angry. ③I am in the cafe.

C is 허준석, is a pilot, My mother(mom) is a doctor

 be동사의 과거형

Part 1

A ①was, were, was ②was, was, were ③were, were, was ④was, was, were ⑤were, were, was ⑥was, were, was

B 본문 35쪽 표를 참고하세요.

Part 2

A ①was, hers ②was, doctor ③was, not ④were, not

B ①Mr. Park was my English teacher. ②Mr. Smith was in the office. ③Andy and his parents were in Korea.

C were, P.E., painting, were

 08 be동사의 의문문

Part 1

A ①Is he your dad ②Was Alex her best friend ③Are they sick ④Were the boys happy

B ①긍정: Yes, he is. 부정: No, he is not(isn't). ②긍정: Yes, he was. 부정: No, he was not(wasn't). ③긍정: Yes, they are. 부정: No, they are not(aren't). ④긍정: Yes, they were. 부정: No, they were not(weren't).

Part 2

A ①Is she a doctor? ②Are you tired? ③Were they late? ④Is she your sister?

B ①Yes, she is. ②No, he is not(isn't).

 09 지시형용사/지시대명사

Part 1

A ①this, that ②these, those ③this chair ④those students

B ①This ②Those ③This, chair ④Those, students

C ①Is this a peach? ②Are these his dogs? ③Is that chair mine? ④Are these students from Spain?

Part 2

A ①That ②These

B ①These ②These ③That ④Those

C ①This is my brother. ②These students are my classmates. ③Is Seoul a big city?

 10 일반동사의 현재형 1

Part 1

A ①X ②O ③O ④O ⑤O ⑥X

B ①begins, feels, gets ②makes, rises, studies ③passes, tries, goes ④watches, does, has ⑤finishes, studies, plays ⑥enjoys, goes, watches ⑦does, passes, finishes

Part 2

A ①listens ②reads ③cleans, his ④brushes ⑤drinks

B ①Kevin ②My uncle ③I

C studies, listens, plays, plays

 11 일반동사의 현재형 2

Part 1

A ①I don't like mango juice. ②Please don't eat or drink here. ③Jessica doesn't like Mexican food. ④She doesn't drink coffee. ⑤They don't like music.

B ①My cousins are baking cookies. ②My dad is watering the garden. ③I am listening to the noise. ④It is snowing outside.

C ①My cousins are not baking cookies. ②My dad is not watering the garden. ③I am not listening to the noise. ④It is not snowing outside.

Part 2

A ①doesn't ②doesn't ③don't

B ①reading ②are, sleeping ③is, crying

C ①studying science ②am fixing my bicycle ③I am playing baseball

 12 일반동사의 과거형 1

Part 1

A ①listened ②looked ③rained ④watched ⑤finished ⑥loved ⑦lived ⑧hated ⑨closed ⑩liked ⑪danced ⑫tried ⑬cried ⑭studied ⑮stopped ⑯dropped ⑰played

Part 2

A ①washed ②invited ③brushed ④played

B ①They danced. ②He closed the door. ③They studied hard for the test.

C ①We planned a surprise party. ②I sang a song.

일반동사의 과거형 2

Part 1

A 본문 59쪽 표를 참고하세요.

Part 2

A ①had ②read ③forgot ④lost

B ①took ②broke ③came

C got, studied, had, made, enjoyed

 일반동사의 과거형 3

Part 1

A ①I didn't(did not) work at the post office. ②She didn't(did not) study hard. ③Michael didn't(did not) use chopsticks. ④He didn't(did not) like the restaurant.

B ①They were playing ②I was using ③It was raining ④We were listening ⑤I was watering ⑥The students were studying ⑦My mom was making

Part 2

A ①Jason didn't go to the hospital. ②You didn't put my wallet on the desk. ③We didn't eat pasta for lunch. ④They didn't visit the shopping mall.

B ①He didn't enjoy the movie. ②She didn't have a headache. ③He didn't live in Brazil.

C 예시답안) I was listening to the radio. / I was studying English.

 일반동사의 의문문

Part 1

A ①Do you speak English? ②Does Jihoo speak English? ③Did she speak English? ④Did you finish your work? ⑤Did Mr. Kim paint this picture? ⑥Did Jane write this book? ⑦Does he take a shower every day?

B ①Do you speak English? 긍정: Yes, I do. 부정: No, I don't. ②Does Jihoo speak English? 긍정: Yes, he does. 부정: No, he doesn't.

Part 2

A ①like ②eat ③live ④bring

B ①Did his family visit Ghana? Yes, they did. ②Did you sleep well last night? No, I didn't. ③Did she go to his birthday party? Yes, she did. ④Did you take a shower after the soccer match? No, I didn't.

 부정관사 / 정관사

Part 1

A ①a car, a school ②an apple, a desk ③a book, an orange ④a computer, an egg ⑤an hour, a horse

B ①The, dog ②the, kitchen ③The, Earth, the, Sun

Part 2

A ①an, a, a ②an, an, an ③an, a, a

B ①a nurse ②ducks ③an expensive car

C ①the ②an, the ③The, the ④the ⑤the ⑥the

 의문사 의문문

Part 1

A ①Who are you? 당신은 누구세요? ②Where do you live? 당신은 어디에 살아요? ③What does he do? 그는 무엇을 하나요(직업이 무엇인가요)? ④When do you go to school? 당신은 언제 학교에 가나요? ⑤Why were you late? 당신은 왜 늦었나요? ⑥Who was his math teacher? 누가 그의 수학 선생님이었나요? ⑦Why did you like it? 왜 당신은 그것을 좋아했나요?

Part 2

A ①What ②How ③When

B ①Whose ②What ③How ④What ⑤How long

 부가의문문

Part 1

A ②isn't, she / No, she, isn't ③is / Yes, it, is ④did, he / No, he, didn't ⑤does, he / Yes, he, does ⑥will, you / Yes, I, will

Part 2

A ①are you, Yes ②does he, Yes ③didn't she, No

B ①didn't, study, English, did, you ②not, there, were, you ③Come, birthday, party, will, you ④likes, blue, doesn't, she

19 조동사 can

Part 1

A ①He cannot speak English. ②I cannot move these boxes. ③She cannot play the flute. ④Mr. Kim cannot fix the problem. ⑤I cannot remember their names.

B ①Can she speak French? ②Can you see the stars? ③Can she play soccer? ④Can Paul swim? ⑤Can he teach Korean? ⑥Can you eat kimchi?

Part 2

A ①My mom can cook really well. ②He can't use chopsticks. ③You can go to bed now.

B ①Can, you, dance ②Can, you, sing ③can, sing, dance ④We, cannot, watch, can, we

20 조동사 will

Part 1

A ①I will not go see a doctor. ②I will not be a scientist. ③They will not come soon. ④I will not go to the party. ⑤He will not bring his lunch.

B ①Will you bring your lunch? ②Will you clean the house? ③Will he eat vegetables? ④Will he drive my car? ⑤Will you visit her place? ⑥Will John love this gift?

Part 2

A ①will, read ②will, eat ③will, close

B ①won't, be ②will, play, badminton ③will, go, to, bed ④will, be, sunny

21 조동사 may

Part 1

A ①약한 추측 ②허락 ③약한 추측 ④허락

B ①He may not be rich. ②It may not be true. ③It may not snow tomorrow. ④They may not be very poor.

C ①May I use the computer? ②May I go home?

Part 2

A ①may, catch ②may, rain ③may, be, sick

B ①May I turn on the TV, you may ②May I wait in the office, you may not ③May I sit down here, you may

22 조동사 must

Part 1

A ①You must not buy a ticket. ②You must not park here. ③You don't have to go there by 6.

B ①Do I have to take vitamins every day? ②Do I have to water the garden today?

C ①강한 의무 ②강한 추측 ③강한 추측

Part 2

A ①must, not, drink ②must, go ③must, call

B ①must, stop ②must, not, smoke ③must, not, bring

C Yes, you, must

23 형용사의 용법

Part 1

A ①cheap ②pretty, girl ③tall

B ①is, expensive ②was, hot(spicy) ③were, long

C ①cheap, bicycle ②pretty, girl, my ③was, interesting ④were, funny

Part 2

A ①teachers, are, smart ②red, car ③is, big ④They, were, honest

B ①Tom is a good student. ②They are clever. ③French is interesting. ④This show is boring. ⑤Alex is healthy.

24 수량 형용사 1

Part 1

A ①many(a lot of, lots of) apples ②much(a lot of, lots of) money ③much(a lot of, lots of) work ④many(a lot of, lots of) animals ⑤much(a lot of, lots of) sugar

B ①much, sugar ②much, money, safe ③a, lot, of, work ④were, a, lot, of, zoo

Part 2

A ①There are a lot of kangaroos in Australia. ②There are a lot of people in Seoul. ③There are a lot of items in the supermarket.

B ①How much money do you have? ②How much time do you have? ③How many brothers and sisters do you have?

25 수량 형용사 2

Part 1

A ①a few, a little ②a few, a little ③a little, a few ④a few, a few

B ①a, few ②a, little ③few, people ④little, water

Part 2

A ①There is some milk. ②There are some spoons. ③There are some eggs.

B ①a little ②little ③few ④few

C ①some ②any ③any ④some ⑤some ⑥some

 26 부사, 빈도부사

Part 1

A ①slowly, hard ②well, now ③kindly, beautifully ④easily, early ⑤fast, happily ⑥carefully, late

B ①very ②early ③carefully ④never ⑤fast

Part 2

A ①He speaks Chinese well. ②I get up late. ③Jason walks slowly. ④Look at the book closely.

B ①can play the piano well ② can run fast ③exercise(work out) every day

C ①My mom often gets up late in the morning. ②I never use a red pen. ③He is usually late for school. ④I will always love you.

 27 what / how 감탄문

Part 1

A ①What a nice day it is ②What exciting games they are ③How handsome Mr. Kim is ④How fast the horse runs

B ①How smart she is! ②How delicious it is! ③How diligent he is!

C ①What a cute cat it is! ②What a kind boy he is! ③What tall buildings they are!

Part 2

A ①What ②How ③How ④What ⑤How ⑥How

B ①How ②How, expensive

C ①How difficult the question is ②How noisy the kids are

 28 비인칭 주어 it

Part 1

A ①날짜 ②요일 ③시각 ④날씨 ⑤명암 ⑥거리

B ①비인칭 주어 ②대명사 ③비인칭 주어

Part 2

A ①It, cold ②It, 2:45(3 to 15) ③It, July

B ①is April ②is Saturday ③is sunny ④It is 2 km

 29 시간을 나타내는 전치사

Part 1

A ①at, at ②in, at ③in, on ④in, on ⑤on, in ⑥in, in ⑦in, in ⑧in, on ⑨in, in

B ①at ②in ③on ④in ⑤in ⑥in

Part 2

A ①studies, on, Sundays ②home, at ③enjoys, in, winter ④go, school, in

B ①I went to the movies in the morning. ②He reads books at night. ③My father was born in 1970. ④She doesn't eat anything at night.

30 장소를 나타내는 전치사

Part 1

A ①in ②on ③above ④next to ⑤in front of ⑥behind ⑦under

B 본문 127쪽 그림을 참고하세요.

Part 2

A ①She is in the living room. ②It is on the desk. ③It is in my bag. ④She is behind the curtain.

B ①There is a gas stove in the kitchen ②There are a lot of computers in his office. ③They were born in Gwangju. ④I met him at the airport. ⑤He is taking a walk in the park.